THICK as GLUE

Annette Gaston

Olympus Story House

Table of Contents

ACKNOWLEDGEMENTS...I

INTRODUCTION II

THE REJECTED ONE 1

GRADE SCHOOL EXPERIENCES 4

CHILDHOOD AMUSEMENT 6

PLAYTIME AT THE DUMPSTPER AND CORNER STORE 7

THE DEATH OF MY FATHER 8

DISOBEDIENCE I GOING TO CHURCH 9

BANNEKER JUNIOR HIGH.....................................10

FIRST TEENAGE FIGHT 12

CARDOZO HIGH SCHOOL 14

BOWIE STATE COLLEGE 16

MORGAN STATE UNIVERSITY 19

MY FIRST APARTMENT 20

CENTRAL MISSOURI STATE UNIVERSITY 22

WESLEY THEOLOGICAL SEMINARY 24

MISSIONARY EXPERIENCES IN AFRICA 25

MY EXPERIENCE COMING TO MIAMI........................36

MISSIONARY EXPERIENCES IN PORTUGAL 38

MISSIONARY EXPERIENCES IN TRINIDAD 45

CARNIVAL IN TRINIDAD, A NIGHT OF TRAGEDY 46

EVERYDAY LIFE IN TRINIDAD 48

RETURN TO THE UNITED STATES 53

TURMOIL AT "505" 60

RENTERS AT "505" 70

MAINTENANCE HELPERS AT "505" 82

OVERALL VIEW OF RENTING AT "505" AFTER THE
CHRISTIANS AND DEMONS LEFT. 85

I WAS USED AS A "VESSEL" 88

CONCLUSION: PRAYER AT LEISURE MOMENTS 90

ACKNOWLEDGEMENTS

Dreams come to those who have faith and perseverance. Never let go ofyour dreams, no matter how your situation looks.

I would like to dedicate this book to those people who inspired me constantly when I almost gave up, especially my friend, Meredith Hunter, who constantly, for years, motivated me to write.

I would like to thank Pastor Ruth E. Crockett who prayed constantly for the venture with me.

I would like to thank Pastor Rich Wilkerson, Trinity Church, Miami, Florida for giving me hope and inspiration to write this Story.

My mother, Laura Bell Gaston, always told me God works

mysteriously in your life if He has a purpose for you. She had to raise four children on her own; it was this strength that kept me pressing on.

I would like to thank my sister, Annie Gaston, who stood by my side for eighteen years, supporting me emotionally, financially, and spiritually.

This is an autobiography of a missionary who went through

the challenges Of love, betrayal, racism, and poverty—from childhood to adulthood.

INTRODUCTION

This is a story about a young girl Of seventeen who came from the ghetto of Washington, D.C. Sitting on her porch, she had a dream at seventeen that life had to be different than what she had experienced. This young girl dreamed of traveling to different places. It is a story of a domineering husband who was determined to break racial barriers among white denominations around the late seventies to early eighties. It is a story about the successes and defeats that a young, independent black couple went through on the mission field, living in different foreign countries. It is a story about how white missionaries r elated to us. It is a Story of how we were blended around the world. We found out just how the different countries reacted to us. It is about the challenges that I had when I reached the United States of America.

On December 13, 1955, l, Annette Gaston, was born, along with my nvin sister, Annie Gaston, at D.C. General Hospital in Washington, D.C. Growing up during my early childhood years; I lived in a raggedy one-bedroom apartment at 1125 23'" Street, N.W., in Washington, D.C. from 1955 to the 1960s. My mother's ame was Laura Bell Gaston. She was a typical homemaker, and my father's name was Augustus Gaston; he was a barber by profession. My mother and father were strict on us. All of us shared this one-bedroom apartment with my brother and sister. It was such cramped quarters; there was no privacy for anyone. When I turned eight years Old, my mother had a baby whom she named Delores. This made the one room even more crowded.

When I was very young, I did not understand why my sisters, Lana and Inez lived across town with foster parents. My mother would tell me that my father did not treat them well because they were stepchildren. Our family was poor, and my father did not provide suffciently for the children. He used to beat the oldest child, Inez. Inez had problems living in the house. Sometimes, she would play hooky from school.

He did not beat Lana because she was pretty with long hair. My mother said she had to make a decision to give them a better life. So she placed them in foster care. I never understood why. I guess since my mother was not educated to hold her own, she felt that was the right decision. Even though she was not educated, she was a beautiful woman and knew it. She told us as kids she looked like an Indian even though she was African American. She had black curly hair and a reddish-brown complexion. My mother would make trips to the foster parent to visit them. She would attempt to buy personal things they could use. She had to save the small amount Of money Our father gave her.

Since my father Was in the military, he was very strict He wanted my retarded brother to grow up and become a barber. He even kept all the barber equipment from the military. Since my brother was born mentally retarded, this shattered my father's dreams. My father would take my brother Mancie on fishing trips with him. It seemed to me that my father was mean to us girls because he was so disappointed about my brothel's condition.

My father was African American with a light brown complexion and gray eyes. My mother called him "cat eyes" when she got mad at him.

My brother, Mancie Gaston, was born January 15, 1953, and died July 17, 2001, of a massive seizure. It looked like there was a Curse Over him because it seemed as though something negative was always happening to him. When he was a baby, he had a hernia on his stomach that required surgery. After his birth, my mother found out he was not responding to Sensory things like other babies. The doctor diagnosed him as mentally retarded. My mother said before he was born that she was too active. She said when she was carrying him, the house had a back porch that did not have steps. My father did not have money to repair the porch.

She would leap down when she had to use the yard to take trash out and hang clothes on the line. She would have to leap when she Was pregnant.

I had to do a lot of chores around the house, and I had to go to the grocery store. I experienced embarrassing moments at the Supermarket, because we could only afford pork and beans for dinner and hot dogs. We even had to wash clothes by hand. We had no washer.

I remember not having a childhood, because we did not have birthday parties; my family could not afford them. I had to learn responsibility at an early age. I had to sign my own field trip forms in elementary school because my mother could not read well. She would lecture me about getting an education. She did not want me to end up like her, just having children.

THE REJECTED ONE

I would describe Mancie as having big eyes. It seemed as though he was surprised about life. He was a trainable person, and he could communicate in a sentence and remember people's names. But he was rejected by the children in our community. The children on our street would meddle not only with Mancie, but with the entire family. They would throw rocks at my brother and call him names. When we sent him to the store, people would take his money.

We would not tell everybody at school, even in our junior and high school, that he was mentally challenged because we did not want to go through the abuse of children making fun of us. I did not let my girlfriend, Hope, know until high school. She did not understand why I kept it a secret. When my brother got older, he would take walks outside to get out of the house. He would be tired Of sitting in the house with my mother looking at TV all the

When we moved to 14th and T. Street, N.W., Washington,

D.C. in the middle seventies, the neighborhood had a lot of crime. I even witnessed a man getting killed in my neighborhood for pushing drugs. The neighborhood had all types of people— drug addicts, alcoholics, and prostitutes, and some working people. He began socializing with men standing around the liquor store, and the men turned him on to alcohol. It got to the State of dependence, and he started having tremors and seizures. He was admitted several times to the hospital. My mother said on One occasion that he came up missing for two weeks. A neighbor said he got in a van with some people. She reported it to the police. He was gone for two weeks and returned back home. He did not go   into detail about what had happened to him. All he said was that thefd blindfolded him in a house, and he was thrown into a room. It gave my family the impression that they had molested

Years later, he was hit in the knee by a metro bus. He developed

1

arthritis in his knee and walked with a limp. That slowed down the activity of running across town, and he started staying in the house more.

Before his death in 2001, he had three seizures and a stroke. He was Only forty-eight years old. In June, my sister, Annie, and I visited D.C. together for the first time. Usually, I stayed behind and manned our house in Miami. This trip seemed like a special trip for some reason. My twin kept telling me, "I am so happy you didn't stay behind. We got a last chance to physically see our brother for the last time." When we got back to Miami, we received a call telling us he had died a few days after he got admitted to the hospital. It was meant to be by God. There would be no more tears, no more crying, and no more pain; God knew his suffering.

When we saw him, he looked very sick and had lost weight. We went out to buy Our mother and brother some ice cream. It y,ras a gallon. He ate all of the ice cream up a nd did not save anything for anybody. My mother made a statement I will always remember: "l hope that he's not dying, because my mother was craving things before she died."

I thought, Why would she make such a statement? Yle said our goodbyes to my mother and my sister Delores. We said goodbye to Mancie and hugged him. He said goodbye back. After we reached Miami, in the same week, we got a call from our sister Delores that Mancie had fallen out and hit the floor. He was unconscious. He had been rushed to the hospital. He was in a coma. My sister and I prayed to God that he would come Out of it. But he did not. We had to board a plane in Miami and rush back to Washington to a funeral. For economic reasons, we had to cremate him.

I believe God is a just God, and He knows when we are constantly suffering. He knew that Mancie was a forgotten One in his life. Mancie had gone home to another life where people are not born mentally retarded but made whole. He's probably looking down at us and feeling sorry for what we have to go through on earth. At moments, I often think about him, but there is peace and happiness. Revelations 21:4 says, "And God shall wipe away all tears from their eyes and there shall be no more death, neither sorrow nor crying, neither shall there be any more pain, for the former things are passed away."

GRADE SCHOOL EXPERIENCES

I started grade school in 1961. I remember the day my mother had to take me to school. My sister and I started school at six years Old because my mother did not have proper clothes for us. My first elementary school Was Stevens Elementary School in Washington, D.C,, which was not too far from my house. In the morning, my sister and I would walk to school with our peanut butter and jelly sandwiches.

I loved school, because I was studious. Because I was studious, a girl in the classroom did not like me. I made stars on my papers when I did well in class. I did not like violence and did not have it in my home life. She was big and a bully. She was very dark-skinned. One day, she hit me in the coat room, and I hit her back. I did not know how to fight. All of a sudden, I was just swinging my arms like I was swimming. The children in the classroom said I won the fight. My sister, Annie, did not help me because she was afraid, too.

I remember the teacher would play the piano in the classroom, and I was so afraid and timid. My sister was the only person I would talk to in class. Some of the students were hostile at times. The students would make fun of our attire and say, "Your mother needs to buy you all better clothes." They would tease us about our clothes, because they were thrift-store clothes.

One day, I came home from school, and my mother told us we had to move out of the one-bedroom apartment. The housing authorities were tearing it down and constructing a parking lot for more parking space for the steak restaurant.

There Was an extravagant steak restaurant across the lot. My mother would watch the people dress up and go into the restaurant, and she would daydream about a steak dinner.

In 1965, I went to Park View Elementary; I was scared to go to another school because of the children. They mistreated us because we had a men tally retarded brother. In the meantime, my brother had problems getting into school late. During the 1960s, the school system did not have a lot of special education programs. One day, I saw my mother just sitting in the chair weeping over him. She was trying to get him in school because she did not want him to be idle, without an education.

We left 1125 23rd Street, N.W. and moved to Rock Creek Church Road in Washington, D.C. This section was upper Georgia Avenue, N.W. I attended Park View Elementary School. My teacher's name was Ms. Oliver. She was a very stern teacher and did not let the children play around in class. This was a primary class, and I stayed with this teacher until the sixth grade. There were some tough kids who liked to fight, and she would take them in the coat room and beat their buttocks with a paddle.

I felt protected in this classroom because Of the teacher. The children continued to ridicule us because of the way we had to dress every day, because of our thrift clothes. We never wore new clothes. I remember the field trip to the White House to See President Johnson speaking. Chairs were placed on the White House lawn. He was speaking about staying in school and obtaining a good education. I ran home to get my mother to sign the field trip form. Over the weekends, my mother went to a thrift store to buy me some shoes for the event. The day Ofthe field trip,

I was so happy. However, everybody in my class had on new clothes. I felt out of place, and a student in my class made fun of my shoes. I started to cry, and I did not enjoy myself at the White House.

I was so uncomfortable because I was not dressed properly, and my mother could not do anything about it. I felt sorry for my mother, too. Even though the students made fun Of me and my attire, they did not realize I was Very smart in my lessons. I remember a girl stood up in the class and named all of the smart people in the class. She called out the twins and also a girl named Rosemary who had long hair and was part Indian.

CHILDHOOD AMUSEMENT

We did not have fun playing like Other children. We lived a serious life. Our parents did not have money to buy us toys all the time. Therefore, we played amongst ourselves. During my childhood, I was not privileged to have a birthday for my twin sister and me. My mother could not afford to buy a cake for us. The only party I knew of was at school. At Christmastime, the Salvation Army would bless us with toys. We would be So surprised when we woke up in the morning. I was excited just going through the toys in the boxes. Most of the time, we needed money for food because my father was retired. We would play amongst ourselves, my sister, my brother a, nd l. We did not have too many friends because of the way our house looked inside. The furniture was beat up, even though it was clean. When we would go to the playground, I would swing so high to forget my problems.

PLAYTIME AT THE DUMPSTPER AND CORNER STORE

When I was outside playing with my friends and sister, when we had money our mother gave us, we would buy lollipops, chips, sodas, and candy. When I was seven years Old, my sister and I and a girl named Debbie would go to the corner store. There were a lot Of goodies at the corner Store. Mother did not have money to give us all the time. The corner store had a first-floor level with side steps that led to the basement. Down in the basement was where all the sodas were kept. The store would throw away pies wrapped in boxes. The things that they did not sell, they would throw away.

The pies were lemon and apple. My sister and I knew the best time to go to the dumpster. It was at night. We would dig through the trash and find boxed pies and eat them. That was Our dessert for the evening. We had a girlfriend named Debbie who lived upstairs. She also liked the corner store. She would go to the corner store and take items. She would try to convince me to do it, but I was too afraid. I ran so fast from the store and did not tell my mother.

Debbie even taught me bad things to do that my mother did not know about. Debbie was only seven, and she said that she had a boyfriend. She asked me if I had one. I said no. She asked me if I ever kissed a boy. Debbie said she would train me how to do so. So, she held my head back and kissed me on the mouth. It felt so strange to me.

She was always in trouble with her mother. One time, she took her mother's money and spent it at the corner store. We were buying candy and everything in sight. She got a beating when her mother found Out. Debbie moved Out Of the apartment, and my mother was glad.

THE DEATH OF MY FATHER

While living on Rock Creek Church Road in our two- bedroom apartment, one night, I remember my father being very sick. The ambulance came and took him to the hospital. The next day, the hospital called and said he'd died of heart failure. Our father died May 9, 1968. We Were twelve years old. I remember he lay in the bed about two weeks sick. His health had turned worse. The next day, he was gone. My father was twenty years older than my mother. My father did not believe in God. He never looked at a church building in his life. I had been told that if you did not believe in God, you were an atheist. I guess he was an atheist. He retired a few years before he died. Basically, he would watch Mancie, my brother, and he loved boxing On TV. I really did not get to know my father because he was stern and very distant with us since we were girls.

After he died, One night, I saw a vision of him looking me in the face, and then he vanished. When my father died, my mother was left with four children to raise on her own. We had the help Of the Social Security Administration. For some reason, people would come into Our lives to give my mother money for food. This must have been God, the person they talked about at church. I know now it was God. God was sending His guardian angels over us. Even though my mother had disagreements with my father on certain matters, I believe she loved him. She wept horribly at the funeral. I did not cry. I felt a big lump in my throat.

Since my father was in the military, the Veterans' Administration helped to pay for his burial. We rode in a black limousine, at the cost Of the government. The military shot bullets over the casket. We rode home broke after the funeral. We were now a single-mom household.

After my fatheds death, I wrote a poem about Heaven. It was a touching poem, and it came from my heart, because I did not know anything about Heaven.

DISOBEDIENCE I GOING TO CHURCH

My mother was ashamed to go church because she did not have pretty clothes. She would talk about how the church people would look down at your clothes with a frown on their faces.

So, church was not a part of my life as a child. My mother was a Baptist as a child and would lecture me about going to church and told me that God would bless me as a child. I cannot remember seeing my mother ever going to church in my childhood or as a teenager.

I did not want to go church. I wanted her to go with us. I was a stubborn child at times. The most spiritual person in the family was Aunt Molly. She would ask me every Sunday if I"d gone to church. She talked a lot about getting saved and having your soul right with God. Then she would put two pennies in my piggy bank. Aunt molly would get on my mother"s nerves, because she did not go to church.

After my father died, a friend of the family took my twin sister and me to church for the first time at age twelve years old. It was a Baptist church. The people in the church were clapping their hands. Some were crying and talked about the goodness of God. It was such a strange experience to me, and when I returned back home, I asked my mother what was going on in the church. I did not understan. My mother said, "it"s the Holy Ghost that gets into people." Then she raised her voice and said, "You need to go to church on Sunday."

BANNEKER JUNIOR HIGH

My sister and I graduated from Park View Elementary School. We went to Banneker Junior High School in Washington, D.C. in 1968. Banneker was an inner-city school. It was predominantly black. I remember having all black teachers.

At Banneker, I was going through the adolescent state. I was going on thirteen years old, and I started thingking about a boyfriend because I saw teenage girls dating. I even noticed girls getting pregnant. She would tell me not to talk to bad children. Children were not allowed to visit our house. Most of the time, I would watch TV and read my school books. I could not wait to go to school to read the books. It was an escape from my lowly home problems. I would often daydream as I read the books.

Some of the teachers at Banneker had low morale because of the social problems with the black students. There were a lot of fights at school, and I was afraid. There were several girls who looked like they controlled the whole school. When my sister and I would go to the store across the street from the school, the children would ask us for money. Then they would say, "Take off your shoes." They would check our pockets for money. We would be obedient and did as they said. Even the black principal could not control the girls. At times, there were plate fights in the cafeteria. We would run for safety under the tables.

The black teachers would try to uplift the students constantly about getting and education, and they would tell us stories about the Deep South. They would talk about the lynching of blacks and how people were hung because they were black. I used to have so much fear in my heart about the Southern states. There was one striking teacher named Ms. Cabbage. I was taking an English course from her at Banneker Junior High School. She was white American. She would sit in class and talk about every subject but English. One day, she told the class to write a short poem. I wrote a poem about when you love somebody, you don't go by looks, and as love grows old, you still love that person.

When I was a teenager at school, I used to be fascinated with people's life stories. Ms. Cabbage would read stories to us, and I would picture the characters in my mind. When she told the story, I would get.so excited just thinking about it. The black students would complain and say that the class was not teaching anything. I recall one time she told us to write what we wanted to do in life. I wrote that I wanted to become a writer. She gave me a lecture and said, "It is hard to become a writer because you have to be extra good." Then she commented, "I don't think you should go into that field." I felt disappointed again.

Some Of the white teachers had an unconcerned attitude toward the black students because there Were So many behavioral problems. Students would cut classes and yell into the door during teaching. But some teachers cared about us. However, it did not Stop me from wanting to be a writer.

It Seems as though I made friends with the downtrodden at an early age. Hope was still my best friend at Banneker Junior High. She was a large-built girl, and a lot of the students made fun of her, especially the boys. Hope made all A's and B's in school. She did not have a boyfriend. I did not have one because I was too

One day, Hope asked me if I was going to college. I told her my family was So poor, my mom couldn't afford to send me. Hope's mother had two years of college. Hope wanted to become   an architect. Since my friend wanted to go to college, it caused me to begin to think about going to college more seriously. I wasn't motivated by my mother, because she had no idea what higher education was about. She thought if you were poor, you Went straight to work after high school.

FIRST TEENAGE FIGHT

I never was a child that liked to fight, but I remember one fight I was in. One weekend, a girlfriend named Hope and my sister, Annie, decided to go to Malcolm X Park in Washington, D.C. It was a huge park in Washington, D.C. Malcolm X Park would have bands come to play, and singers would come to perform during the summertime.

One day, we were walking through the park and came across three teenage girls sitting on the bench to the left of us with a puppy. The puppy ran out, and my sister, Annie, accidentally stepped on his paw. We begged their pardon. The girls did not want to accept our apology. They cursed at us and called us a bunch of dirty names. The girls were average weight, but not fat. Two Ofthe girls had dark skin, like Africans. Hope, my girlfriend, encouraged us to talk b ack to the girls. So we talked back and ended up getting into a fight with the girls. We were under the impression our girlfriend would help us out, but she did not. So we got beat up badly in the park. My sister refused to rub the puppy s toe because of pride. We tried to fight the best we knew how. All I know is one of the girls hit me in the eye, and I fell to the ground. I was throwing fists in all directions but could not beat the girl. I saw stars when she hit me in the eye. My sister was thrown to the ground and was pulled by her hair. Hope did not help us at all.

There were some construction men in the parking lot looking at us. They rescued us and told the girls to leave us alone. The girls cursed at the construction workers, but they left. The men said, "Those are roughnecks from the ghetto. You don't know how to fight them. You two 100k like good girls." The men did not realize We lived in the ghetto, too, and could not fight. We only socialized with Hope. We learned our lesson to ignore comments. We were very embarrassed to walk home because Of the dirty clothes. We were sixteen years old. We had ten blocks to get home. Hope went back home with clean clothes on. Our blouses were ripped, and we had dirty pants and black socks.

Our mother asked what happened to us. We were scared to tell the truth. We said nothing. She asked, "Why are you dirty?" We said we were playing dodgeball in the park with some friends. She said, "I have never seen anybody in my life look like you all."

CARDOZO HIGH SCHOOL

My sister and I graduated from Banneker Junior High and went to Cardozo High School, located at 13th and Clifton Street, N.W., in Washington, D.C. When I reached high-school age, my hormones began acting up. I would hear stories about the parties the students were attending. The students told how they danced and had fun while listening to the music. I was disappointed because I could not attend. I was sixteen, and my mother still would not let me have a boyfriend and go places on a date. I was eager to leave home when I grew up.

One day, Hope and I were sitting on the bank near Cardozo High School, and we talked about boys. I told her that I would marry my first love. I talked about traveling and leaving Washington, D.C. My sister, Lana, was a dancer, and she would send us postcards from different cities, like Chicago, Miami, and other cities. On her visits to our house, she talked about those different places. I looked up to her with great expectation and ambition for my life ahead of me, because she was a product of a foster home. I realized how much my mother wanted us to get an education.

In 1974, my sister Annie and I graduated from Cardozo High School. Hope and I had something in common; neither of us was able to go to the prom. Our mother would not allow us to go. My sister and I really had to work hard to Save money during the summer to cover the cost for the robes, the dress, and pictures for the graduation. My Oldest sister, Inez,, showed up for our graduation. My mother told her to go to support us. My mother did not go to the graduation. She had a complex about her hair and clothes.

We received our diplomas. It Was a beautiful experience, because my mother had gone to only the eighth grade. I felt since I was grown, I could live a better a better life since my mother could not afford to give it to me.

Hope and I were discussing our college careers. I told her that I wanted to go Out Of state, just to get away from all the home life that I had to put up with during my high school years. My home life seemed So terrible to me because Of the strict behavior pattern of my mother and then the terrible poverty issue. I just wanted to go to college in another state to get away from it all. It was my childhood dream that I envisioned.

BOWIE STATE COLLEGE

My sister and I went out of state. My first year of college was at Bowie State College in 1974. The college was far out in the woods in Bowie, M. D. This was my first time away from home, and, Ofcourse, it Was very interesting to me. The college consisted of mostly black students. The teachers were black. Even though the school was in the woods, everyone enjoyed it. My mother was not thrilled about us going to college. She thought We wanted a social life. She asked us if we were going to meet boys and run around. She Wanted us to go to work. We were a bit rebellious about this.

However, We had to be very careful who we associated with because a lot of the students were getting through college using drugs. They smoked marijuana a lot on campus. My mother did not have money to send me, and I relied on financial aid from the school. As 1100k back, I see that that was God's gift to us.

My twin sister, Annie, and I went to the same college together. The first year, we did not get a room together. I had two roommates in my room. One young woman they called Feet" because she was very short and wild. A lot of boys liked "Two Feet." My roommates knew I was very shy, but they said I Was a nice person. Some ofthe students said they did not want to be there, but their mothers sent them away to school, and they had no choice.

I never got acquainted with the party atmosphere at Bowie. My first party was quite a shock to me. I had to learn how to dance. When I was dancing with the boys, my heart was just racing and beating fast. I never Was close to a young man before. I was scared and excited. Drugs Were something new to me, and I started coughing from inhaling the smell of the marijuana, and then I found out they were smoking reefer.

One day, I was in the lounge where the girls did their hair. A big guy tried to talk to my sister, Annie. He was popular on campus and was in many activities. The students called him Coco because of his dark complexion. It was at Bowie State College that Coco became my husband. coco mistook my sister for me and later dated me.

I remember my first date. We went to the movies to see a karate picture. I just stared at the movie. I could not look Coco in the face. I was so shy since this was my first-time experiencing dating.

He was very smart, and he would help me with term papers. He made good grades. He was in the honor society because he made A's and BSS. Coco was a social work major, and he was always listening to someone's problems and counseling them. He was a senior, and I was a freshman. A lot of the girls became jealous of me because I was dating a senior. He played football for the school. On one occasion, he told me that football was his god. He would talk to me a Iotabout his life as a teenager. One time, he told me he'd almost overdosed on drugs, and how God saved his life. Coco said that he was wild as a teenager. He hung around with the wrong people. We talked about a lot of things, and he told me his grandfather was a Baptist minister.

In his last year of college, he Came to my dorm room and said he wanted to discuss something with me. His message to me was that he wanted to become a pastor of a church. At that time, he was twenty-one y ears old, and I was eighteen years old. I was shocked at the time, and I asked him if he was sure Of his decision. He told me very seriously that he definitely wanted to be working in a church as a pastor.

In my heart, I realized that being a pastor's wife would mean a lot Of responsibility. He even broke the news to me at that time that he wanted to marry me. He looked at me through serious eyes and said, "l believe you would make a very good pastor's wife." Of course, this was all new to me. I didn't know what to say. I wondered if I could be a good pastor's wife. How would I know this?

Coco graduated from Bowie and went on to Wesley Theological Seminary in Washington, D.C. Because I had never belonged to a church as a child, I could only remember the stories that my mother had told me about the church. I had really Only visited church once or twice. My mother had said that a lot of politics went on in the church with the different committees, and she even went so far as to tell me that some ministers were doing wrong things. I used to wonder why my mother was nagging me about the church if there Was So much going on that Was not right. She told me about some Of the pastors and to tell the truth, I did not know what to really believe.

MORGAN STATE UNIVERSITY

I left Bowie State College and went to Morgan State University in Baltimore, Maryland in 1975. I still had my mind made up to major in English. After the first literature course, I dropped the class. The school seemed harder than Bowie. A lot of the students failed classes in the English Department. I had been told that they had the best English Department in the city. I decided to change my major to sociology because I had a lot of curiosity about different cultures, and I enjoyed talking with people from different nationalities.

Many times, I felt like dropping out of college because 1 did not have any support from my family. At Morgan, some of the students' families had money, and it was obvious to those of us that were from a different background. Some Of the students would ignore me and treat me like a poor person. I had to work summer jobs to support myself for books, travel, and snacks. I did enjoy college, even though I suffered much ridicule. It was interesting meeting people from the different states. My teachers made the classes very interesting. I had to learn the entire map of Africa in one class. At the time, I never thought I would ever travel to Africa, but I became the first missionary at Morgan State's Sociology Department to travel to Africa in 1979.

We were approaching our last year Of college. Times were really getting harder and harder for us. We were under pressure to graduate because we were only financially funded for four years. My sister and I had other responsibilities, Such as paying rent on the apartment and buying food. The only savings we had was through summer jobs.

We graduated from Morgan in May 1978. AS usual, my family did not show up because they did not have proper clothing and transportation. I was unable to show up at my own college graduation because I did not have all the materials needed. In fact, I could not even buy a cap and gown. We packed our clothes and got out of Baltimore, Maryland. We moved back to our mother's apartment, in Washington, D.C

MY FIRST APARTMENT

I was tired of living on campus at Morgan State University. The campus had begun to get boring to me. The partying and the roommates started getting on my nerves. At age twenty-one, in our junior year, my sister, Annie, and I moved out to an apartment complex called Argonne Apartments in Baltimore, Maryland. The neighborhood was one of middle-class working black people. Our apartment had one bedroom. My sister, Annie, and I shared the one bedroom. We had twin beds in the room. The only problem with the apartment was that we had a leak from the roof area located in our bedroom. Therefore, when it rained during the summer, it would start leaking in our bedroom. Whenever it rained, we prayed it would not be a hard rain. We had peace during the winter months. The Owner was taking advantage Of us. He would not repair the leak The apartment was affordable. We used our part-time jobs to pay the rent. We were working on the college campus. We went out and purchased used furniture to decorate the place. We would invite a few Of our college friends to Our place to study and look at TV shows with dinner.

Across the hallway from us was a man in his thirties. He called himself Tammy. He was a homosexual. One day, he asked us if we were twins. We responded, "Yes." We had never experienced having a friend who was a transsexual. We studied a lot about his character and behavior. We did not discriminate against him for his behavior. He was very intelligent and initiated all kinds Of intellectual conversations. He liked to cook a lot and gave us food. He liked fashions. He would observe our hair and fashions. On the weekend, he would dress up as a Woman and try to tell us to get Out more by going to a club. We would never take his advice. What amazed me was the number of attractive men that would visit him and go On dates with him. He would walk out the door, twisting, with a short miniskirt and a long wig on his head. I asked him where he met the guys, and he would Say, "In prison." One unfortunate thing that had happened to him, we learned, Was that his mother had put dresses On him because she wanted a girl. We eventually moved out of the apartment to a better one.

CENTRAL MISSOURI STATE UNIVERSITY

After my graduation from Morgan, I wanted to continue my education. My fiancé did not want me to go to graduate school. But, I had always had big dreams of being an educated counselor working in the prisons. Coco tried to talk me out Of pursuing my career because he wanted to become a pastor Of a church. But I had my mind made up. I enrolled in Central Missouri State University in Warrenburg, Missouri, along with my sister, Annie.

I landed in Warrensburg, Missouri, in November 1979, in a town I had no knowledge about. We finished college at Morgan in 1978. We decided to go to graduate school, but we did not know where to go. We saw a short program at Central Missouri State University for criminal justice administration. We jumped at it. We told One another we would have a master's in a year. My fiancé, Coco, drove us from Washington, D.C. Out to the college campus in Warrensburg, Missouri. When we got to the town, we experienced a cultural shock. We felt like turning back but could not. The university was in a small, conservative town. The school was predominantly white Americans. Since We had come from black schools all our lives—elementary, middle school, high school, and a black college—we had a sense Of insecurity as to whether we could do well at the university. We had heard a lot Of myths about blacks going to predominantly white universities and how difficult it Was for them to perform because of their socioeconomic background. Somehow, Annie and I managed to take the classes together. Most of the time. we would be the only two blacks in class. We would never talk but listen. I never heard the kids make any racial remarks while we Were on campus. We made friends with a girl named Marilyn. She was biracial. Her mother was black and her father Was white. Marilyn had a Very social personality, and she was a nutrition major. Life seemed so lonely to us because we were so far from home.

Since I was raised up in Washington, D.C. and that was during 1960s and 1970s and at the time, it was mostly a black city, I'd never heard the racial term, "Nigger." One night, Marilyn and I decided to go to a club. This was where the college students hung out. A group ofwhite American boys in a car yelled out the word, "Nigger." I was stunned and in disbelief. I did not realize how the word "nigger" hurt so much and how little I'd feel. We did one year there because I was going overseas with my husband, Coco, to Africa.

WESLEY THEOLOGICAL SEMINARY

Coco was attending Wesley Theological Seminary and Came in contact with an African American professor while taking his course on religion. In this course, one learned about different cultures around the world. In the class, among Other things, students would sample different foods. This professor seemed to like my fiancé and was helping him with his career. coco would talk about what went on at the seminary. He said some of the students were racist and made fun Of his weight. They would tease him in his preaching class, and they would ask him if he was going to "preach black that day" and whoop and holier. Of course, the white culture had a different concept of church services, and the students were not taught that all cultures do not worship the same, but all people should be honoring the same God. This was around the year 1976.

The black preaching style was not accepted in some site churches. One day, Coco's professor asked him if he would like to go on a seminar trip over to Zambia, East Africa. So, that summer, when school was closed, he went over to Africa. When he came back, he was a changed person. He said, "I want to become a black missionary, because there are very few on the mission field." I did not know too much about Africa, except what I saw on television, Tarzan and the natives. I remember the movie Roots gave us some insight.

MISSIONARY EXPERIENCES IN AFRICA

I was viewed as strange among some religious leaders because I was a black missionary who started out at the age Of twenty- three in 1979. African American missionaries were very few. Our first mission field assignment was with the Methodist Church, and I saw very few African American missionaries in the organization. Then, I transferred to the Presbyterian Church in 1980. This church was one percent black on the mission field. This was a Very conservative church.

Very few African Americans on the streets of the USA have met black missionaries who traveled abroad to different countries during the era We were doing missionary work. I am talking about the ones who eat different foods and live around different cultures and speak foreign languages.

Furthermore, Some white Americans a nd religious leaders felt that blacks were not capable Of living around different cultures and learning foreign languages to communicate with different cultures. Some Of the white missionaries would be so amazed at us. They just were not used to black missionaries.

By then we were engaged, and I was working in Indianapolis, Indiana, as a youth counselor with the summer youth program. My fiancé finished his seminary education and flew over to Sierra Leone, West Africa. In 1961, Sierra Leone became independent from British rule. It was a free colony for free slaves after slavery. Coco was appointed to a church as a pastor in the village of BO. He made preparations for us to get married in the capital of Freetown. Bishop Bangura, who was the Bishop Of the Methodist church, organized the wedding.

When I left the USA in September 1979, I did not have any idea what I was getting into. Africa was viewed as Such a mysterious continent by researchers. It was called the Dark Continent. In September 1979, I boarded the pan AM Jet to Sierra Leone, West

Africa. I was excited and at the same time, scared. I went alone. It was a seven-hour trip by plane. My first stop was Monrovia, Liberia, where my luggage transferred out. The Liberians had a unique accent. They spoke so fast, and I did not know the procedures at the airport. Everything looked so out Of order. It was a Canadian traveler that showed me through the airport and where to pick up my luggage. One had to be careful not to have his luggage taken.

Before I boarded the plane to Sierra Leone, I watched the Liberians just jammed at the airport window. They were looking at the travelers. Some of them had sad faces, some smiling faces, and others had a look that they wanted to travel. Going to America or somewhere else was paradise to them. They did not know their land was full of riches and wealth. I landed in Sierra Leone, West Africa in September 1979. As I approached the door of the plane to walk down the stairs, a wave of humidity hit my face. My face felt scorched. Moments later, I became very dehydrated from the climate. I became very thirsty for water. The airport was very primitive. They did not have water fountains. I had to buy bottled water.

I saw black people all over the airport. They were assisting theinternational people with their luggage. Furthermore, Sierra Leone had a black president. I felt extremely proud when I heard that. A black president was a taboo in the United States. The Africans were very dark-skinned in complexion. They had flat noses and thick lips. I was used to seeing African Americans with many shades Of skin complexion—fair, light brown, medium brown, dark brown, reddish brown, and dark.

I said in my mind. "I am back home. I am in the motherland. I wonder where is my tribal linkage? Why was I born in America?"

When I got to the airport in Sierra Leone, my fiancé Was waiting for me. It was so hot. My body had to adjust to the heat. I caught a taxi from the airport to the capital and drove up into the mountains. As I rode through the streets, I saw so much poverty, poverty worse than in the United States. I started feeling guilty. I was blessed to be born in America. America gave me the opportunity to obtain my high school diploma and further my education into college. These poverty-stricken people did not have any opportunity.

I know God sent me to these poverty-stricken people to give them hope, faith, and lead them to the lord.

On top Of the hill Stood a white missionary house. I stayed there before the wedding. October 6, 1979, Was the wedding date. There were missionaries from all over the world at the wedding. A missionary couple from Sweden baked the cake.

After the wedding, We moved to our new home in another City called Bo, Sierra Leone. Bo was a small village city. We lived on the Methodist Church Compound, and down the road was the church where my husband pastored.

Some of the white missionaries would just sit around and talk about how the Africans were stealing. We lived next door to a white missionary couple from Denmark. He did not want the indigenous Africans in his house. If a marketer would come by his house selling something, he would scream so loud at them to get away.

The Sierra Leonians loved my husband's preaching style. The Africans were so amazed at us, because they were used to seeing white missionaries. One man just stood and looked at my husband and said, "You a black American," with a smile.

Some of the Africans even said, "Welcome home. We have heard about the prejudice in your life in America. Some Africans were conf sued and addressed us as white people because we were living around whites in America. I was viewed as a white woman by the people in the village because I was light complected. I feel the African American is bi-cultural. Many historians believed that black Americans did not have a culture until Alex Haley wrote Roots

Some religious leaders did not want to believe that blacks were not accepted in some white churches over twenty-five years ago. In the village of Bo, life was simple, and you would wake up in the morning hearing the rooster crow. The village had a lot of snakes in the woods at night. At times, there would be an electricity shortage in the village. All of a sudden, all the lights would go out. One would have to use a flashlight to get around. The men would run from the snakes. The women were the brave ones to kill them. They would set the bush on fire.

I can See why the black American woman is strong. It is in Our roots from Africa. I would just watch the women walk down the dusty road with wood on their heads. Village life Was traditional, compared to the big city. Out in the village some of the women would go topless. In the big city, Freetown, the women would dress western style. Some women even wore jeans in the city. Pants were not worn a lot in Africa. A lot Of the women did not have jobs, even though there were professional women.

It was interesting that the Methodist Church would train native men who wanted to become pastors. These men would come to the USA to study the ministry and get their degree, and some of them would marry village women who did not have even a high school education. These women were very active in the church on women's committees.

The white missionaries would admire how strong these women Were. These women had mental strength out of the world just putting up with poverty. There was courage in the bones of these women. I knew Of one case where one maid moved in the house of a white missionary and it caused problems for the couple. The white missionary lady got jealous, because her husband had an interest in the maid. "lhe white missionary packed her bags crying and called headquarters to leave the mission field. There were a couple of Cases where the white missionary men got involved with their housemaids. Polygamy was rampant among African men, if they were not Christians. Life was hard on the mission field, even for some of the white missionaries in Africa. I knew of cases where white women coped with diseases like malaria. Some even said, "I'm following my husband. What about you?"

I did not want them to believe I could not cope, since I was black in an African country.

One would have to be careful when swimming, because of the risk of acquiring river blindness. Life was hard on the missionary children. There were times when some Of the white missionaries would have to send their children to boarding schools to get a better education. The black missionaries would let their children go to indigenous schools.

The children of Africa were special to me. They had a lot of manners. I once visited an elementary school, and when the teacher came into the classroom, out of respect, the children stood up. There were millions of children suffering from starvation. I watched children live an adult life at an early age.

In Bo, some of the children did not go to school because they did not have food and clothing. Some of these children learned the marketing trade at the age of seven or eight years old. They would be out on the streets selling goods with their mother. One thing I learned was that the children in the USA take things for granted. Seldom did I see a child play with a toy. I did not see toys in the store. I gave a child a book to read, and he was thankful. The children Were taught at a young age to respect their elders. The children out in the village did not wear shoes. They just could not afford it. In the village of Bo, some Of the people practiced tribal marriages. In Africa, a girl becomes a woman between age thirteen and fourteen years old. There were cases where the parents in the village were giving their daughter away to a paramount chief at eight years old. The chief of the village can have one hundred wives. Each wife plays a role in the household. They do not necessarily have to be on speaking terms. There were actual arrangements with these wives living under the same roof.

One wife would cook, wash, and watch the children, and one would do the gardening.

The Sierra Leonians had large families. I talked with one man who had forty children. I could not believe it was true. To the Africans, a lot of children was a sign of being rich and wealthy.

In the USA, when parents get old, some people put them in nursing homes. But in Africa, it is an honor to care for the Old. In fact, grown children planned how they were going to provide for their parents when they got old. If a person does not care for the old, they are frowned upon in the society. The children make preparations while the parents are living.

It is amazing how the USA is viewed as such a sophisticated country, but they do not have the compassion for making provisions for the elderly in Western society.

The religious beliefs of the people were interesting. They were very spiritual, and it is a matter of fact that some believed in voodoo. During my stay in Bo, there was an old man that died. Nobody tried to save his life by taking him to a doctor. One old woman in the village commented that a curse was placed on him.

Sierra Leone had a lot of diamond mines. The Lebanese in 1979 controlled half Of the diamond mines and owned a lot of the businesses in Sierra Leone. There were many poverty-stricken people that would dig up a diamond from the ground and sell it for nothing. The Africans would go to the mines to dig up a diamond and trade it to the Arab Albans entrepreneurs for food at the local store. It was a shame on God's map that some of missionaries Were getting to know the Lebanese to get diamonds and try to find a way to smuggle them into the USA. There was the case of a missionary who smuggled a diamond in his baby's panties to go through customs when he reached the States. In the Keno district. the diamonds were found in the streets. There had been so much exploitation among African people by foreign invaders. Even some missionaries came and exploited the people. The Lebanese would be friendly to us, because we were not Africans.

In fact, some of the Lebanese even bragged to our faces, and one store owner showed us a case Of diamonds he had; he was shipping them off to Lebanon. Some Of the Lebanese became so rich, they owned a lot Of the businesses, and their wives were wearing diamonds on their fingers. Some Of the Sierra Leonians had a low self-esteem about themselves. We would enjoy looking at African pictures and carvings. However, some of the Africans did not even like their Own art.

The illiteracy rate was so high in Sierra Leone that some Of the people did not even know how Old they were because birth certificates were not recorded properly by their parents.

I did volunteer teaching at the Opportunities Industrialization Center compound in Sierra Leone. This program was also in the United States. It was a social program based in Third World countries. The program would teach high school dropout skills, such as auto mechanics and electronics. I was teaching British English to the African students who were affiliated with the Methodist church. English was difficult for some of the students because they spoke Krio, which is a West African dialect. I taught high school dropouts, and my husband gave out scholarship information for students to study in the USA to become pastors.

The government was giving scholarships, but it was difficult to get one if you did not have family members in politics. The children were very smart. had to take comprehensive exams from England to pass high school. The United States is just now implementing the system Of comprehensive exams. The schools did not have all Of the updated educational materials, such as books and learning materials. The missionaries who were teachers brought their material in from the States. The missionaries' children had to adjust to the pressure put on them in the school system. They did adjust very well. They would run around the play and leave the problems up to the adults.

The government hospitals were understaffed, and they were in need of doctors from the States that were highly trained and skilled. The average education of medical doctors was six years. They had to travel to Europe for their training. Some of the women went through natural childbirth. There was one doctor in the town Of Bo who was killing the indigenous people because he was treating them for appendicitis every time they would go to the doctor instead of figuring Out just what medical treatment they needed. I had an African woman friend that knew what was happening on the inside of the Office. I had to visit a government hospital because my eye had become infected, and in the waiting room, there were goats walking around. I found Out that I had been exposed to malaria. The malaria medicine did not seem to help me. so, they gave me hip injections. A lot of the missionaries were being contaminated by this disease. My husband had a strong immune system, so he was able to avoid the sickness.

Local transportation was very tiring; for example, a two-hour trip would take four hours by the government bus. Also, the Sierra Leonians had a transportation van with two benches in the back. It was the most uncomfortable bus I had ever ridden in. At every stop. a person would get on With bags of food, and one man even brought on a live chicken in a basket. The benches were very cramped. The drivers would just speed down the bumpy roads. It reminded me of the Indianapolis 500. It was interesting that the government would pay specialists to come in to do construction work, but there would be tractors just sitting idle on the roads. The government did not have money to train people how to use their equipment.

Much time Was used when traveling the local bus because the driver did not gas up properly. On a trip to Freetown, the capital, the vehicle would run out of gas. The drivers would constantly take breaks along the way. People would get out and talk for almost an hour. They would eat, drink, and use the bathroom in the woods. We were on our way to take care Of business in Freetown, but it was such an ordeal to even get any place you wanted to go I. was reminded ofthe fact that we do not appreciate what We have in the

States. Everything we had to do or wherever we had to go took so much time. This is the way of life in most Third-World countries. When a package would arrive at the post office for a missionary, the Sierra Leonians would pretend that the package Was not there, because they wanted you to give them some money to receive your package. My husband was really against these things. They would try to get money out of us, and he would rise up and be against it. He was willing to let the government officials lock him up rather than give in to the crookedness. I would just stand there afraid and not say anything. I did not know what to do. My husband did all the negotiations. The children also learned how to take a bribe. The USA would send financial aid to the people, and it would get into the hands of government officials.

The Sierra Leonian men were very chauvinistic. I used to watch them out in the village lying under a tree that produced palm wine, which came from the top Of the tree. A lot of Sierra Leone's men were taxi drivers, and they would try to overcharge you for a taxi ride. They did not have meters in their taxi cabs. The men worked at the bank. They seemed to control the money. The average salary was $400.00 a month, with a degree.

Stealing was the major crime in the community. If a thief was caught stealing, they would jump on the man and beat him to the ground. They would yell, "Thief!" and the action began. The police did not carry guns. They carried only blackjacks. For recreation, the missionaries would go from home to home to visit with each other. There was one black missionary family in the country with us. Wayne and Cheryl Maddox became good friends with us, and we would eat dinner at their house and discuss how the missionary women treated the Africans. Some of the white missionaries had superior attitudes toward the Africans. If an African worked for them as a servant, they would try to work the servant to death. Wayne was a construction worker and helped build churches. Cheryl was an ordained minister and religious educator. We would visit the movies a lot with the couple. There were a lot of karate movies imported from overseas and also East Indian movies. We would see a lot of imported black exploitation films from the States.

Sometimes, my husband and I would drive to other towns just to eat out in the village at a restaurant. We ate Out with the village people. They used palm oil in most of the food. Fish, goat meat, and rice were the main dishes. The Africans would eat Out of one plate with their friend with two different spoons. They would drink hot soft drinks. When We decided to follow them and eat out of one plate, they would smile at us. Since we were in the country sharing dinner, everything was sort of primitive. If you had to use the restroom of the tin house, a waitress would take you outside and there was a hole in the ground.

Life was very slow in the village. The women were topless, and nobody thought anything about it. My husband and I would just ride through the village and see the hut houses and people relaxing under trees. One time, my husband went into the village and spent the night. He Was Very adaptable with everyone. To me, the African women were rather hard to get to know. Being an African American woman made them shun me a lot Of the time. They would get mad at you if you did not speak a normal greeting like this: "How the body?" This greeting meant "How are you?"

There was a young black woman named Verna who was born in the USA and remained until age seventeen in the States. Verna's mother wanted to go back home to Sierra Leone. Verna had problems adjusting to the people. She would complain all the time that she wanted to go back to the States. She worked in the Methodist church Office. The Sierra Leonian Women were very jealous Of her because she was born in the States. Everybody thought Americans Were rich.

What was so interesting to me was how black American women were married to African men and gave up their American Culture to go back to Africa. Many of these women became adapted to their new life and had very strong relationships with these men. They gave up all the materialism and freedom they were used to in the States. There were European women married to African men. I knew a European lady who had a biracial Child, but she could not take her back to England with the family, and She decided to Stay in Africa and raise her child.

The malaria kept coming back in my system, and I found it very hard to live in this Country. My husband had to make a decision to leave Africa. I could tell it hurt him. He loved the people. We returned to the States and lived in Indianapolis, Indiana in 1980. He was very angry and dissatisfied. We would get into arguments over leaving the mission field. He received an appointment to a Methodist church in Federalsburg, Maryland. I was only twenty-four years old. I had to learn how to be a pastor's wife in the USA. It was the first time the church had a young couple. The town was Very slow, and church was a big event. We lived in the town for two years pastoring, but in my husband's heart, he wanted to be a missionary, and I could not stop him. I felt so hurt for letting him down. We left the town and moved to Miami, Florida to be appointed to another church in 1981. It was a Presbyterian church in Miami.

The other black couple, Cheryl and Wayne, came home because his wife was pregnant and suffering from hypertension. Cheryl originally belonged to the Presbyterian Church.

MY EXPERIENCE COMING TO MIAMI

My experience coming to Miami was an experience of a lifetime. I used to be scared of the South because of the stories I heard of how they treated the blacks and the Jim Crow laws. When I came to Miami in 1981, there Was a conflict with the police and black Americans. There was a lot of rioting between blacks and Cuban policemen. It was strange to me, coming from Washington, D.C. I thought race relations had gotten a little better. I Was shocked to see the different cultures, like black Spanish people. Up in D.C. during the 1970s, they had a small Spanish population on 16th Street, N.W.

The food was different. They were tropical foods, which I was not used to. Our first foreign population we worked with was the Haitian refugees. The Presbyterian Church made Miami a missionary field because of the influx of Haitians coming over by boat. My husband had to learn Creole to work with the Haitians.

The first house I lived in was a duplex house. I had not seen that type of style up in the North. It was my first house. My first house was beautiful. It had wall-to-wall carpet. It had air conditioning in it. I never lived in anything so beautiful. It was in Miami Shores in 1981. It Was on 108th Street N.E. and Place. The neighborhood was predominantly white. We were the only blacks on the block. When We walked down the street, the white Americans would Stare at us. It was very quiet in the area. I was alone with my husband. I would prepare dinner and clean the house all day. A year later, in 1982, my sister joined me in Miami. She came from Indianapolis, Indiana. I convinced Annie to come because I would brag about the house and the weather. There was an older white couple that lived next door. They Were nice and friendly. They said that we were quiet people. The first church I joined in Miami was New Covenant Presbyterian Church. I had to get used to the preaching because it Was very conservative. The church had a predominately black congregation. My husband was the associate pastor. When he preached, he was doing the whooping and hollering which was done in most black denominations.

Since I had worked for the federal government up North, I got a part-time job at Immigration Services in personnel. I was a clerk typist. It gave me the Opportunity to buy clothes. My husband was trying to boss my money. He would complain when I bought shoes and dresses. He would say, "You don't need that." I kind of wanted my independence and to have my own money. For recreation, we would go to the beach because it was twenty minutes away. Up north, it would take two hours to get to a beach. Miami seemed like paradise to me. At that time, everything seemed too happy to me.

Later, we were appointed to Miami as missionaries. There were a lot of Haitian refugees coming over to the USA in 1981 to escape oppression. My husband became a resettlement officer for the Haitians, but he still had in his heart that he wanted to be a missionary. After searching from here to there, my husband was appointed as a Presbyterian missionary. The Presbyterian Church was a very conservative organization. There were not many black missionaries within this church organization. We were actually the one percent of the black population in the church.

MISSIONARY EXPERIENCES IN PORTUGAL

The Presbyterian Church sent us on assignment in Portugal, Europe in 1984. The Portuguese were the first to start slavery around the fifteenth century. They colonized Angola, which was a Portuguese colony. The majority Of the churches were Roman Catholic. The Portuguese had a strange way of doing business when we arrived in Lisbon, Portugal. They advised us that they did not have our housing ready. The first day in town, we rested at a hotel. It seemed to us that they were not being honest with us. We could not speak the language. The next day, we had to point our fingers at the food menu. The Only thing we understood Was the word "beef' On the menu. They did not have our language training set up. The head of the church drove us up on a mountaintop to live in a cabin for two weeks. It was cold in the house, and the running water was cold. A Portuguese maid came to bring us food. She just stared and looked at us, and I looked at her. It was the first time a black American had been appointed to the church.

The church omcials drove us to the town Of Coimbra. We were the Only blacks living in the condominium complex. My Portuguese teacher was so curious about me. She wanted to know what kind of American food I cooked. She wanted to know what Was in my wardrobe. She even asked me if I had any expensive gowns and jewelry. She Was Curious about my material possessions. We took private lessons under her for a year. The private school Was named Cambridge School of Language, which is a British School. The private lessons were quite expensive, So it was imperative that We transfer to the University Of Coimbra to study Portuguese. All nationalities Were in the class: German, Japanese, and Swedish people from Ireland were in attendance. Coimbra was a college town, and not too many people spoke English. My husband spoke Portuguese well. He had to preach in the native language.

The directors of student housing for the college belonged to the Presbyterian Church. My husband was over religious services, running the budget for the house and giving out scholarships to the students. There were over a million refugees from Angola living in Portugal. The refugees were white and black. When we took over the house, there Were all Portuguese white students living there, but my husband felt that the program should help black refugees also.

We met a student, a black Anglican, who was in medical school at the University of Coimbra. This student was very poor and needed housing. We helped him get a room in the house. He was the Only black. The Portuguese students made up stories that he was stealing food from the refrigerator. They would talk about him negatively. He helped to do business transactions for the house. He was fluent in English and Portuguese. They resented him at the house because my husband gave him jobs to do for him. They could not do anything about it.

The Portuguese students received scholarships for their books. They would to give my husband a hard way to go on every project he tried to work on. Sometimes, they even would pretend they did not know English. But we knew they did. We Were pushed into the job before We mastered the language. We only had three months of language study. With God's help, we accomplished our job.

We were invited out to dinner with the Portuguese ministers. One thing I noticed was that they were not ashamed to have a glass of wine with their dinner. They even bragged that pastors drink in this country. The Portuguese drank a lot of red and white wine. I noticed that the young people, teenagers, started out drinking at an early age. The Portuguese would even make their toddlers sample wine. The average diet for the Portuguese was beef, pork, chicken, and potatoes. There were also vegetables With some Of the meals. A lot of the Portuguese people would suffer from hypertension and heart trouble. What was special about the country Was that they believed in social medicine. Therefore, a person could get treated even if he did not have money.

Coimbra was beautiful and had a lot of hills. It would get scorching hot during the summer time. The Portuguese women were beautiful dressers. They would match colors together that I would never dream of, for example, yellow, purple, and green. They would wear a lot ofbelts with their clothes. wore fur coats during the wintertime. I bought a fur coat during the wintertime. I was the only black woman in the town wearing a fur coat. They were very classy women. They wore diamonds on their fingers. Eating Out was not costly. The food was inexpensive. A big meal would cost only five to six dollars. Not too many black Angolans could afford to eat Out. Sometimes, we would be the Only blacks in a restaurant. Everybody would stop and drop their spoons when we walked in. They would Say, "They must be Americans." They could not believe that we could eat in an extravagant restaurant.

In the town of Coimbra, I knew an Angolan female doctor who owned a car. My husband was the only one in town who owned a Fiat, a French car. The Portuguese people would get jealous When they saw us in the car. They even kicked the car one time. They called my husband a nigger and asked what We were doing in a Fiat. Sometimes, we were driving on the streets, and they would try to run us off the road because we had a new car.

We would tell the incidents to the Portuguese church officials, and they would try to convince us that the Portuguese people were friendly. It had some validity. We even had some Portuguese friends. They were very curious about black Americans.

There were some basketball players who did not make it to professional in the USA and went overseas. These Portuguese girls wanted to marry them to make it to America. I went to one basketball game to look at the Americans and see how they played on the team. It was interesting that these black American guys learned the language well without taking training to study.

One black American dated a Portuguese girl and ended up marrying her. One black American dated Only Portuguese women.

There were Other missionaries in the country. We met a couple from Norway and ate dinner at their house. The Norwegian couple was curious about Americans. There were black Angolan women with light complexions married to white Portuguese men. There were a lot Of light-skinned Angolans and Mozambique people. The lighter the woman, the greater the tendency was to marry white Portuguese men. It was a sign of class. The Portuguese people would always confuse me with the light-skinned Africans from Angola. They did not say bad things to me. I do not know whether it was because of the color of my skin. In some countries, people place emphasis on whether you are mixed, which determines how you are treated. We were the only black American couple living in a condo in the building in Coimbra. The Portuguese were so amazed at us. They thought my husband was an engineer. The Children in the building would call us monkeys. What made it so hilarious was even Some white missionaries could not adjust to the Portuguese culture. The Presbyterian Church sent a white missionary before us to Portugal. The white man could not adjust to the Portuguese. He ended up packing his suitcase and leaving. He could not adjust to their way of thinking.

I was alone most of the time in Coimbra. I would just clean house and study. I had a Portuguese maid. The maid's salary was six dollars a day. I believe that she was so jealous of us because she would always say Americans had money.

When I got tired of the house, I would go shopping. The clothes and leather s hoes were very inexpensive. I became a friend to a young woman from Zaire. She would braid my hair. It was difficult to get your hair done at the salon. They did not have black salons. So, I went to all white beauticians. They washed my hair and tried perming it. It would not Come Out right. My hair was so thick for them to handle. Some of the Africans had curly hair that just required washing and drying.

The Latin people believed in visiting people late at their house. Someone may visit you up to twelve o'clock at night. The crime rate was low. Some of the women would walk through alleys at midnight. People would be on the street eating and drinking. They would sleep late in the morning. Some even got up at twelve o'clock noon. The businesses would close down at noon, and they would have a two-hour rest break.

It was interesting about work ethics. The women, ifthey could not find a babysitter, would just bring the child to work with them. The Portuguese had a superior attitude over the African refugees, but some of Portuguese did not have manners in public. If a child had to use the restroom, they would pull the child's pants down in public. Even in front Of a restaurant when you were eating.

We met a Portuguese man who owned a radio station in the town of Coimbra. He was interested in black spirituals and blues. so, he talked to my husband about playing black spirituals on the radio station. And my husband agreed. He was also interested in black American music and black spiritual singers. My husband organized the radio station. My husband wanted to inform Portuguese people about black American music. The program was talked about all over the town of Coimbra. It was a success.

My husband started acting strangely to me one day. While we were attending the University Of Coimbra, we met an Arab girl from Montpelier, France. This girl would visit our house and eat dinner with us. For some reason, she did not talk to me a lot. Everybody would Cater around my husband. We would help pay her tuition at the college. I believe she was going behind my back getting money out Of my husband. She wanted us to go to France. She was in Portugal because she was an exchange student. I was twenty-nine years old then, and my husband was talking about my having a baby. But I was not ready for a child. I even thought about going back to the States to work But I was having problems with my ovaries. I would be in a lot of pain. So when the summer came, we went up to Montpelier to visit the Arab girl, but I still had a strange feeling about this young woman. We stayed on at the University of Montpelier in France, vacationing. One day, my husband asked me if I wanted to camp out. I said no. He said that he was camping out by himself. Somehow, I stayed in the dorm room crying because I believed he was with her. The next morning came, and the Arab girl and my husband knocked at the door. She wanted to wash her face. Then I knew she had camped out with him. When we got back to Coimbra, he talked about a baby, and I could not have one. He even talked about divorcing

One day, a letter came in the mail from the Arab girl. I was curious and opened the letter. My husband found out that I opened the letter. He was so mad that he became enraged and threw me across the bed and hit me on the arm. At that time, I had to make a decision to leave Portugal, but I thought about how we would look in the eyes Of headquarters where we worked. He even told me to get out, and I did not have the money to fly back to the States. I called my sister, Lana, and she said that she was not going to pay my way back to the States. So, one night, he just left the condo and said he was going to France, and when he got back, he had to make a decision about me. Whether to divorce me for this girl. Therefore, I was left alone in the condo crying for two days, holding on to my Bible. Two days passed, and he came back and said he found her in bed with another man. Then. he asked me to forgive him, and I did but it looked like my world was tumbling down. Then there was the racism we Were experiencing from the Portuguese people. So, we had to settle our problems for the sake of the church. There was pressure On us to perform on the mission field because we were the first blacks.

So after all the confusion, he apologized and I forgave him Of the affair. He started trying to please me by spending more time with me. We would go to the movies a lot. The Portuguese loved American movies. They would admire the lifestyle of the Americans. Because Of some films that showed Americans living well, they thought all people lived like that in the States. The Portuguese did not have a lot of large people in that society. In the movies, when they saw a large person, they would burst out laughing at the person. I had to put up with them making fun of my husband's weight. The country was beautiful. If you were mixed black, that would make a difference. I was viewed as a mulatto. The design of the city was beautiful. Portugal had some modern-looking buildings and apartments. The houses looked Old on the outside, and when you went inside, they were beautiful. The Portuguese loved gardens. Everywhere you went, they would keep up their gardens.

It was amazing about the educational system of Portugal. In the Portuguese culture, if a person had a bachelor's degree, one would address him or her as a doctor. I had to get used to addressing people with a degree as doctor. The Portuguese loved going to bull fights for sports. The only thing different was that they did not kill the bull like the Spanish bull fighters.

The Presbyterian seminary was a small seminary in Lisbon. Coimbra became unbearable for us. Then, we moved to Lisbon, thinking it would get better because it was a larger city. I taught ESL (English as a second language) to the seminary students. We were running out of things to do because the church officials were not cooperating with us.

Because of the racism, we had to call headquarters again. They had empathy for us and said it was hard keeping missionaries in Portugal. My husband got drained and tired trying to cope with the racism. So, he wanted to leave Portugal. Therefore, the Presbyterian Church appointed us to Trinidad, West Indies in 1986.

MISSIONARY EXPERIENCES IN TRINIDAD

The director of the Caribbean office had to negotiate with the Trinidad church for a black American to be appointed. Trinidad was about 50% black and East Indian. There were other minorities such as Chinese, French, and British. The Presbyterian Church in Trinidad was populated with a congregation of East Indians. We made history because they had never had a USA black appointed to an Indian church. I noticed a lot of the black Trinidadians were in politics and the East Indians owned most of the businesses.

Trinidad and Tobago are islands in the West Indies. They lie in the Caribbean Sea. Port of Spain is the nation's capital, largest city, and chief port. The East Indians were brought to Trinidad to work on the Sugar plantations and decided to make this land their permanent home. The white missionaries set the church up for the East Indians. I noticed that the East Indian women were not vocal in politics and had very little opportunity to voice themselves in the church. It seemed as though the East Indian society was male-orientated. Some women were just content raising children and housekeeping. It Was very difficult to carry on conversations with these women, because most of them had no idea what the rest Of the world was all about. They would just talk about cleaning house, cooking, and raising children and participate in small talk.

We were appointed to a church in Sangria Grande, Trinidad. The church members would come over to our house. The women would separate from the men because the men would talk about intellectual subjects. These women did hold Sunday school 54 classes as teachers in the church. We only stayed in Sangria Grande about a year because there was a group of people trying to run the church themselves and did not want my husband to lead them. They did not want to submit to authority.

Shortly after we left this church, my husband was offered a church in Mirabella. My husband took this church with a big congregation to pastor. This responsibility grew until my husband and I were over nine churches in the city.

CARNIVAL IN TRINIDAD, A
NIGHT OF TRAGEDY

Carnival in Trinidad is a big event in February. People save up money all year round to buy costumes. On the night of carnival, a friend named Tara came over to the house to get me to go to a carnival party. At first, my husband did not want me to go with Tara to the party. He was meeting some people who were in town down from New York. So when night came, he went with the people. I went with Tara to the carnival party. There was a lot of dancing at the party, and people were eating. It was nice. So we left the party about I a.m. at night. When I reached back home, all the lights were out in the house. The door was broken into, and the dog was gone. It was dark outside of the house. I tip-toed into the house; the bars Were broken. The drawers were left open with papers thrown on the floors. Clothes were rummaged through. Knives were lying Out on the table in case someone came

in. The TV was stolen. The house was on a dark hill. I called the police, and they said it was too late to come Out. The back door bars were broken. I was so shaky and nervous, and my husband Was nowhere in sight. So I fell asleep at 7:00 a.m. with the house open. The police and my husband showed up in the morning. I shouted at him and asked where he'd been. He grabbed me and said, "You are alright." The church members did not know I was left alone all night until morning while my husband was out in the streets. I was in tears.

My twin sister, Annie, came to Trinidad to visit us for Carnival. My sister observed quite readily that the people were not Very friendly to tourists, especially those from the States. Trinidad had a lot of hills, and their houses were built up on the hills. The black Trinidadians loved to party On the weekend. Calypso music was playing all over the streets and radio. The people played steel bands. They started playing steel bands at a young age.

The Carnival is a major event in Trinidad. Poor people would save up their money all year round to buy a costume.

The month of February was carnival season. People all over the world would Come, even some movie stars. people would be dancing on the street. The missionaries would try to go somewhere where it was quiet. At this particular time, a lot of houses Were broken into, especially the homes that belonged to foreigners in the country. They would break in and steal everything, even your clothes. As far as social problems existing, there was a lot of unemployment and much crime. The jails in Trinidad were terrible, and the prisoners were treated very harshly, and some prisoners were even hanged.

EVERYDAY LIFE IN TRINIDAD

However, the East Indians were very ambitious people. They had high goals they wanted to meet. They were hard workers, and their children followed in the father's footsteps striving to learn from him. It was amazing how the young people wanted to accomplish their goals, and if they thought they were not doing their best and moving forward like their fathers, they became very discouraged. Some even wanted to take poison and commit suicide if they were not successful in this area. My husband had to deal with these families about many particular circumstances.

I cannot even explain the loneliness that I suffered during this period oftime. I would become too insecure because my husband was so caught up in the people, and he neglected his home life. The pastoring took so much ofmy husband's time that he had no time left for me at the end Of the day. To be able to accomplish some things in my own life, I began taking piano lessons under a Trinidadian teacher. It was difficult for me at first to learn the technique, but it gave me something to be interested in and helped to keep me busy. I wanted to be doing something useful with my life.

At this particular time in my life, I met a girl named Tara, and She introduced me to the American Women's Club. The majority of attendees were American. I met black American women who were married to Trinidadian men. There were also white women in this club. The ambassador of Trinidad would give tea parties, and the women would sit around talking about what they liked about the country and the different cultures.

It was interesting that I also met a woman from Lexington, Kentucky, who was divorced from a black Trinidadian. She ended up living in the country. She said that she did not want to go back to the States. She was not working, and it was difficult for her to deal with the unemployment problems in the country. However, she liked this country because it was slow-paced, compared to the

States. It was so interesting to me to see how many black Americans could give up all materialism and yet adapt well in these Third-World countries.

We began to meet different people which became an asset for me. My husband and I met a woman named Margaret. I don't remember her last name, but she was very interesting. She retired at seventy years old in the States and went overseas. I could not believe that She was living alone in a foreign country. Margaret had family problems with her grown children in the States. She was a very assertive individual and into everybody s business. She went to Kenya and got kicked out for talking to the women about politics. Adaptation was no problem for her. She would walk with a cane to get around and hop buses to cultural events. Because she was so different and interesting to talk to, I became wellacquainted with her, and I could talk to her about my likes and dislikes in this country. She seemed to understand me, and at this point in my life, I really needed a friend.

One day, my husband and I went with Margaret to the beach, which Was up in the mountains. She discovered this beach and invited us to go swimming. While We were in the mountains, we decided to invite her to visit Our church in Mirabella. She wanted to meet the East Indians to see what their culture was like. We shared some intimate moments with her in regard to these people and how diffcult it was to pastor them.

A lot Of the East Indian men would become familiar with the black Trinidadian women, and many of them would become pregnant. Most Of these men Were married, and when the babies were born, these men would not claim them as their children. These children were cast out of the East Indian families because they were mixed.

Some of the East Indians did not accept my husband as a pastor because he had dark skin. They did not want a black pastor over an Indian-majority church. Some would talk about his skin color, and many would refuse to shake hands with him. In Trinidad, if anybody had an inch of straight hair, they would be classified as an Indian even if they were of African descent. Some of the Indians looked like Africans because they had Negroid features. For instance, many of them had the African nose feature. It was confusing to me to distinguish the African from the Indian, and this was important to be able to do so as not to arouse friction among them. My great-grandmother was an Indian.

Sometimes, I would hate to walk out of the door, because of the harassment Of the men. They were flirtatious. I really did not know how to deal with them on that level. I wanted to be friendly, but many times, they would try to take it the wrong way.

A typical East Indian meal was Curry chicken, goat, rice, and roti. We would eat the curry patties with beans and curry rice. I even learned how to cook curry in my household. Life was very slow in Trinidad. People would get up early in the morning. Someone would come to your house before eight o'clock in the morning. I had to adjust to getting up early. We would jog about 7:30 in the morning. In the back of the house was a Presbyterian school for the Indian children. My husband would give motivational lectures at the school.

We would take some time Off just to get away for a vacation, and we would visit the capital, Port au Spain, and take a tour to visit the sights. The workload here was very taxing, as we would have to answer the telephone calls and counsel the members about their family problems. In Mirabella, the East Indians opened up a nursery for low-income children to attend. The Africans could not go to this school.

Many ofthe East Indian men had alcohol problems, and so we set up a counseling program to help them. These people were attracted to my husband's preaching style. They would comment that he was a dynamic preacher, because he would relate the scriptures of their life situations. He would motivate them and tell them they were somebody special. They needed encouragement in both the natural and spiritual elements of their lives. Our main ministry in this city was pastoring and counseling.

The congregation was composed of Hindus who converted to Christianity. These East Indians had beliefs that were traditional, even though they were living in Trinidad. The families still chose and arranged their daughters' marriages. Some younger teenagers Were fighting trying to break from this tradition. The women had to pay for their wedding to the groom. There were cases I read about in the newspaper where some men would kill their future wife if she could not come up with the dowry (wedding). I noticed when they would get married, they would choose a spouse close to their skin complexion. A dark East Indian would get married to a dark woman.

We began to have problems in our marriage, and it seemed to be caused by all the racism on the mission field. My husband became disturbed with all the problems, and he began to change in his attitude toward me. To my surprise, one day, I became aware that he was having affairs with the Trinidadian women. NO wonder things were wrong at this time. I found a gift that he had purchased for a Trinidadian woman, and when I told him about it, he became very angry. I imagine the fact that I found out about it caused him to react in a very ridiculous fashion as a pastor. After all we were Pastors and our life had to be above reproach at all times. He was so angry with me that he beat me up and broke up the furniture. He began to abuse me and treat me harshly in his anger and sin.

I would beg my husband to let me return to the States. He would not let me go because he was determined to make history being a black missionary. I was so sad and ashamed Of my husband's behavior that I started having health problems, so I decided to leave him by himself in Trinidad. My sister, Annie, was living in an apartment in Miami, and she told me to come back and get a job in the States. When he reached America, my husband ended up marrying the woman he had the affair with.

When we left the Country, an article was written up in the newspaper about the racism we encountered as a couple. This article even indicated the church just Was not ready for another culture to minister to the members in Trinidad. The article told about the derogatory Statements they made against him as a leader and pastor.

RETURN TO THE UNITED STATES

When I got back to the USA in March 1988, I was totally drained and stressed from the treatment I received in the Third World. I did the most I was allowed to do being married to a man who only wanted to make a name for himself. I gave nine years to the ministry and was not able to use any of my educational skills or my master's degree in counseling for the prisons.

I went through a divorce on December 8, 1988. It was the chauvinistic behavior of my husband that caused me to become confused and disappointed. I had tried the hardest and longest that I could assist him in the churches on the field, but he refused my help because he felt he was the important person in this marriage. My husband did not want to believe that Women had a right to use their education and potential, but they were only to be subservient to their husbands.

I could not take it anymore. I became ill a year after I entered the United States. I was hospitalized for depression at Southern Winds Hospital in Miami, I suffered from a lot of guilt because Of a marriage that failed and also because I blamed myself and believed that I had failed as a missionary. The enemy started talking to my mind, telling me that I was a nobody in the sight of God. I believed that pastors were not allowed to get divorces because of their positions in the church, and that no matter what took place in the church, they had to stand strong in all adversity. Because Of my husband's infidelity, I believed I was able to get a divorce, but the enemy had played such a trick upon my mind that I became confused. I was ashamed to tell people I was divorced from a pastor. I felt helpless and lost. What was I going to do with my life? I was thirty-two years old.

While I was at Southern Winds hospital, I met the nicest psychiatrist, who treated me for my condition. Dr. Edward Georgia was so kind. I had never had a White doctor before this time that treated me with so much love and compassion. I felt drawn to him, and he told me God could have returned me back to the States for a reason. The doctor said that since my sister had a baby, maybe my purpose for returning to the States was to help her. She had nick named the baby Junior.

During my sickness, I became even closer to God, and I depended on Him to heal me and bring me through this terrible trauma. I needed God to give me the answers to my problems, and I realized that He was the only one that could and would understand me. I have learned how to have a personal relationship with Him.

I have always felt that I have a mission in life: educating people in my culture. I even consult with different people about becoming a missionary. Over the years, I have Seen churches make progress in the USA, and African Americans are now welcomed in their congregations. We were not allowed to have this privilege twenty years ago. There are many mixed cultures in churches today, some with white and some with black pastors. People today are interested in learning each other's cultures. I feel that if the black missionaries overseas were represented on religious television stations here in the States, it would make a big difference in the attitude of the foreign countries.

Even though I had left the missionary field, I was still praying for them, and I have never lost the vision that I once had for those people that I pastored along with my husband. I suffered so much on the mission field, but life for me away from the mission field Was difficult also. It was like I lived in a protected life in the church. Some of the church people were friendly, and others seemed to have an attitude. Most people were not friendly. My attention was drawn to my career, and I was seeking to find out what I should do for the future. The depression kept me from thinking Clearly. I had to figure out what I was going to do with my career. I was so depressed.

In my search for employment, I realized that I was limited because my only experience was working in churches. The majority

Of that experience took place abroad, so I became discouraged because I was very limited in my skills, even though I had received my college degree. •lhe only experience I had was international work and volunteer teaching.

One day, I was job hunting and a female pastor told me about the state government. I found out that they were hiring people with college degrees. I was referred to the HRS in Miami. One day, I came in contact with a church member that my former husband was acquainted with. His name was Mr. Tolbert. Through his help, I became an employment counselor for HRS. I worked with women who received public assistance. The supervisor's name was Mary Cope. She was very kind and always had a smile on her face. She made me feel at ease, and I do believe this woman knew that I did not have a lot of experience. She was very supportive of me and told me she felt I could learn the job. The job was interesting, and my position was to find employment for the clients. It was also part Of my duties to assist the Clients in working with their barriers. Even though some Of the clients seemed hostile towards me, I endeavored to work with them and to enable them to become successful. The inner-city clients were the ones that seemed to feel inadequate around me because of my education. I prayed and asked God to give me the words and wisdom to deal with them. And He did!

Because of my sincerity and willingness to work with people, God blessed me with my first professional job. I could not believe I had my own paycheck in my hands. I had to adjust to the environment because it was the first time I was employed with African Americans. The black women did not understand me because I was always alone. They did not realize that I had gone to the mission field at such an early age and had to be alone so much Of the time. During that time on the missionary tour, I became afraid to trust people. I did not mean to be aloof or stuck- up. I just was not used to a lot Of associations. This I had to learn quickly in order to mingle with my coworkers.

The young women would make fun Of my dresses and tease me about wearing them so long. I was having trouble making the placements, but the supervisor worked hard with me, and she did not fire me. When I made decisions, the other counselors were not supportive of me. Most people said that I acted differently; however, some people did like me, especially the clients. I believe I seemed different to everyone because of my background. Going overseas so young, suffering turmoil and agony from my husband, feeling as though I had failed God in my missionary effort, all these things had taken a toll on me, but I was determined to stick to my work.

Even though a lot oftime had elapsed, my divorce was soon to be final. I had a nervous breakdown On the job, and my supervisor was right by my side. The nervous breakdown changed my entire life. I was running in and out of hospitals for two years. The psychiatrists did not understand why I was there. It was a mystery to them, but I realized that the long, tedious grind that I had endured took a heavy toll on me.

It was the first time I had to take medication for depression. At times, I did not know what I was doing. One night, I jumped in the car and went driving to find a friend's house and got lost. I was speeding, and the police caught me. He told me that I was speeding, and I told him I was lost trying to find a friend's house. He looked at my license, and I told him I used to be a missionary and was trying to write a book. He just laughed at me and let me go. I would become confused as to where I was going, but I could always remember my sister's telephone number and name

On One occasion, I ran outside with my gown On and walked down the street in my area in Miramar. A white man was driving a car alongside of me, and he stopped. I just jumped in the car, and he took me over to his house. He said his wife had left him and he gave her everything. He came Close to me and tried to touch my breast, and I ran out the door and walked down to the next house. I just sat down. A black couple came to the door and asked me if

I was Okay. They asked me into their house. They had beautiful furniture, and I started admiring how their house looked so pretty. I touched the silverware. The lady called my sister. My sister could tell that I was not coherent. Then they took me to the hospital, and the worker acknowledged that I had been there before.

I became so depressed, and I stopped going to church for two years. Of course, that was what the devil was trying to do all the time. The devil hates the fact that We love God and depend upon Him for everything. people would tell me to go back to the church, but I did not want any part of the church. I just wanted to be an average person and let my hair down, as they say.

I started to date at thirty-two years old after the divorce, but it was not easy when I had spent my entire life, from an early age, With one man. I met a guy who lived in the North Miami area near my sister's apartment. He lived on the next street. He was very tall and nice-looking. He told me he was separated from his wife, and he was a counselor for HRS (Human Rehabilitative Services). He was from Baltimore, Maryland. He began working in my Office for Project Independence, and his name was Danny. This man made my life miserable by standing me up every time we planned a date. So I ended up leaving him. I even started going to parties, but I did not smoke or drink. I was a very unhappy person, without purpose.

My husband abandoned me after the divorce. He went on about his business and got married. It was a shock to me after nine years Of devotion. He was disturbed over what took place on the mission field. He did not give me his phone number, so I did not know where he was. I was left with a $3,000 income tax bill that he was supposed to pay. I had to go live with my twin sister again. It took me eight years to pay the Internal Revenue Service. I came in contact with a young woman named Diane who worked for HRS with me. Diane spoke to me about going back to church. We would read scriptures together on the job. She began talking to me about God, and I began to listen to her and what she had to

Say concerning church. It had been so long since I really wanted to believe again. Many times, we strike Out at God when He really is the only source we have to help us. She told me God an take away any illness you have. One Sunday, I visited with her at the Pentecostal church. I used to look at her tithes and notice how faithful she Was in her giving. Sometimes, she actually could not afford it. Diane said she could not afford to pay her tithes.

My husband had told me stories about some black ministers and what they were doing in the local church. He had such a vicious mind about everybody but himself. He never wanted me to believe in anyone but him and his work. One day, he told me some terrible things. He said that he had seen pastors dip elderly women in their bath tubs with water from the faucet and call it holy water. These women had illnesses and needed healing. They would get a hundred dollars from these elderly people.

Diane Was the inspiration that caused me to have confidence enough to go back to church. However, I still had to go back to the hospital because of panic attacks. Eventually I found it hard to Stay on my job because I was too nervous to do the caseload. I worked for HRS for two and half years.

At this point, I was having problems with my brother-in •law-to-be, Ricky. He wanted to put me out ofthe house, and I did not have a place to go at this time. There was so much arguing going on over me that my sister ended up putting him out of the house twice. I recall that my brother-in-law got in an argument with me, and my blood pressure went up so high I had to be hospitalized again. It seemed to me as though I Was going to die, and God was coming for me. At the hospital, they gave me some medication and I went into a trance. It seemed as though I was at peace in the trance. When I woke up, the mental health worker asked me how I felt and I replied that I had died. The worker burst out laughing at me. The mental health workers were positive in their helping me. My counselor told me to believe in God and put my hands on the Bible and say these words: "I won't return back to this place again." She said to believe and it would happen. The counselor prayed for me that night because I was so scared. He encouraged me by telling me that he had seen people that really made up their minds not to go back and got well. I had also seen people make up their minds and refuse to come back

The mental health hospital reminded me of a prison. They let you go outside for a short time. people were looking at TV all day. All day you watched people just go over and over their problems. The patients would support each Other. I saw compassion in these sick people's hearts. They came from all walks of life: poor, rich, educated, and illiterate. They all read Bibles and prayed a lot. Some cases were worse than others. One woman fell in love with a man, and when he left her, she became mentally disturbed. Some Of the patients would just run in and out of the hospital. The workers knew their names but acted as if they did not care about them.

I made up my mind; I Was not going back to this hospital. I just detested taking the medication. When I left my counseling job for six years, I tried to get Social Security disability. The Office would turn me down every time.

I ended up one day at the HRS (Human Rehabilitative Services) food stamp line and became a client. All of the lavish lifestyles came to an end. The workers at HRS Were mean and snobbish. They thought everybody that walked through wanted a life Of ease by being on welfare. They to realize that some of us needed the Stamps to exist. I had to adjust to this new lifestyle. I would ask God. "Why me, Lord?" I even felt I 'Vas not worthy to God. I felt like I was a dirty rag in His eyes. I know that is not true because God loves us all in spite of our sins, shortcomings, illnesses, diseases, and in whatever State We might find ourselves. He is a loving and forgiving God. He is present to answer us if We Will just call on Him.

TURMOIL AT "505"

After a long ten-year relationship with ups and downs, my sister, Annie, decided to get married to Ricky in 1995. They purchased a house in North Miami, Florida, with an in-law quarter to the rear. I lived in the in-law quarters. The house was ideal for two families, because it was a big house. The house had separate private entrances. I was able to enter through the rear Of the house. The house had a huge yard. One could build an additional house on the land. It was a blessing to Annie and me, because we never could afford a house up north in Washington, D.C. All we knew about was apartment life.

They purchased new furniture for the house. Furniture was purchased for the living room, dining room, and kitchen. For my in-law quarters, I purchased nice used furniture. nut's all I could afford with my part-time job. It was the first time I felt some independence since I was in a private area of the house.

They took trips to Washington, with their son, Junior. Ricky never left me out Of the vacation trips.

When they went out to dinner, I Was always invited. We would frequent Red Lobster a lot. We would pig out, because we could afford the meals.

When I needed money, Ricky offered it to me. Most of the time, I could not pay it back to him. Unfortunately, I tried to work but could not h old on to a job, because of my stressed immune system. I was on a lot of anti-depressants, and I felt like a zombie going to work.

I know that I placed a lot of strain on their relationship, but there was nothing that I could do. I could not move in with my mother in Washington, D.C,, because she lived off a fixed Income.

In Florida, a single woman does not quality for public assistance if she does not have a child. Social Security turned me down several times. My Sister refused to put me Out on the streets.

We were bonded at birth. If she had done that, it would have disturbed her mentally. But I believe God placed me with them to help with my nephew, Junior. I attended to him a lot when he was a baby. I picked him up from the daycare daily while they were at work.

Ricky got tired Of the burden. Another person's burden can Wear you out mentally. I believe God put him in Annie's life to carry me as a burden. Maybe God knew it would have been too stressful to Annie to take care Of her baby and take care Of me at the same time. The Bible says in Galatians 6:2, "Bear one another's burdens, and so fulfill the law of God."

I believe Ricky got so tired Of me he started using me as a scapegoat to take advantage of Annie.

Later on in their marriage, Ricky started getting close to Annie's friend Katherine. He was always concerned about her needs, because she was a single mom. Katherine had known Annie for about ten years. Annie had a lot of respect for her, because she went to church at least every Sunday with her child. She had invited my sister to church on many occasions. My sister accepted the invitation. Katherine always Cried about not having a husband in her life. Her child's name was Shirley.

Ricky accepted the appointment Of "goddaddy" for her daughter. He felt sorry that Shirley did not have an active father in her life at the time. She was about ten years old at the time.

Katherine always talked about God all the time when the subject matter came up. Katherine devoted her life to Shirley. She pushed her daughter to model. She pushed her daughter to get involved in sports. Katherine placed a lot of self-esteem in her 72 daughter. Unfortunately, Shirley had never met her father as a young child.

Katherine talked about wanting to get married all the time. She acted like she envied married couples. She frequented the homes Of married couples all the time. The women of the married men felt sorry for her. They would send their husbands to do work in her house; for example, one Of Katherine's friends was a mechanic. He would fix her car when it broke.

On one occasion, when Katherine needed her house painted, the same mechanic helped to paint the house inside. His wife sat in the house and watched him at work. Ricky wanted to help out with the paint job. Annie did not understand why he wanted to help paint Katherine's house. Annie told him, "You need to paint our house first. This house requires a lot of painting." To prevent a big argument, Annie said, "Go ahead over there to Katherine and help her paint her house." When he got there, the mechanic was painting the house. Katherine told Ricky that she did not need any more help.

There were always needs that Katherine had. She was an independent woman, because she had a good government job. She was not a public assistance case. Furthermore, she was an attractive black Woman. She was built very thin. I did not understand why she could not get a boyfriend to help her with these problems.

Annie trusted Katherine because Of the long years she had known her. She was very naive. Annie looked at the fact that Katherine went to church. We never saw men hanging out at her house since she was a single mom.

We found out Katherine was very deceptive and used "Jesus" to get what she wanted. The Bible says, "Beware of false prophets, who come to you in sheep's clothing, but inwardly they are ravenous wolves. You will know them by their fruits." Needs just started coming in from Katherine all the time. One time, her car was in the shop. Ricky and my sister picked her up from her house for two weeks to take her to work. On another occasion, her television blew out. We had five televisions. We lent her one.

On many Occasions, Ricky would go to the grocery store and deliver food to her house. She would call Annie and say, "Ricky is over here." Annie would tell her to stop letting Ricky into her house. Katherine made the statement, "At least I let you know he is here."

Annie told her, "You got to have respect for me."

Annie started arguing with Ricky about jumping to Katherine's needs. He would not listen at all. He told my sister, "I am sorry, if my goddaughter has needs I have to respond to." He told Annie that she was selfish.

He also said to Annie, "You take care of Annette." Again, I knew that I Was a scapegoat for his lustful behavior towards Katherine. I felt he was using revenge against Annie, since I had lived with them so long.

I believe Katherine was feeding him information on what not to do for me. I believe Katherine was basically jealous, because they were married. In addition, they were able to buy nice things, because there were two incomes in the house.

The way Ricky was acting, it Seemed as though he was having an affair. Annie did not want to believe it, but the signs were there. He denied it.

Annie got into an argument with Katherine and told her not to come around the house. Katherine was very stubborn headed. She was very controlling. One day, Junior was having his eight-year-old birthday party. There was a knock at the door. There stood Katherine and her daughter, Shirley. Ricky opened the door and welcomed her in. Annie looked at her with a cold- looking face. She said, "l better not."

Annie walked towards the kitchen to get a broom. I ran after Annie. I said to Annie, "Don't do it." Annie was going to take a broom to hit h er. She was fed up with her intervening in their marriage.

After she left, Annie got into a big argument with Ricky. He was still persistent to stand by Katherine. He said to Annie, "I refuse to deprive my goddaughter out of cake."

Annie Said, "Why didn't you just take the cake to Katherine's house? You allowed her to show up at our house. That is

My sister felt betrayed and worthless to him. The Bible says, "For this reason, a man shall leave his father and mother and the two shall become one. " She knew his love for her had diminished.

Katherine kept taunting my sister over and over again. I was beside my sister's side to stop her from getting into the fights with Katherine. I guess I was like a guardian angel.

The next incident occurred, Katherine came around the house with a letter from Ricky apologizing for Annie's behavior at the

birthday party. My sister later read the letter. It said, "Annie is very jealous and selfish. If you need financial help with Shirley, let me know. Annie is accusing me of an affair. I don't know what she does in the evening when I go to work." Katherine showed up with her mother at the door. Her mother defended her daughter.

She told Annie, "l did not raise my daughter to mess with married men."

I spoke out of my mouth, "You don't know what your daughter is doing in Miami. You live in Georgia." I told her, "Leave the married men alone. You are going to end up in death." It seemed as though when we told Katherine to stay away, Ricky s behavior changed drastically. He did not want to go to dinner anymore. He did not want to go out to restaurants.

On one occasion, Annie was trying to get my nephew, Junior, to eat. He was stubborn about coming to eat. Annie and I were in the in-law quarters. Ricky said, "Stop calling Junior to eat in a nasty way." Annie was persistent. I had a male guest at the house in the in-law quarters. All of a sudden, Ricky furiously ran to the back of the house, and he attempted to try to hit her. Ricky had never touched her in their ten-year relationship.

Annie rushed quickly to the kitchen area and picked up a knife, she was so scared. She could only think of his hard fist going against her head. As always, I was on the scene when disturbances broke out. I said, "What are you doing? Are you crazy?"

Annie had become mentally stressed out with him. She had never been violent in her life towards anyone. We have to pray that evil does not tempt us, because one particular action can destroy us. Matthew 6:13 says, "And lead us not into temptation, but deliver us from the evil one. My male friend picked Ricky up by the waist and said, "Man, please don't hit her."

I believe Katherine was still in the background telling Ricky how to destroy the household. Annie had told him she wanted a divorce. He made things get worse around the house.

The next demonic thing he did was he kept Junior Out Of school for eight days. Annie could not drive him to school, because she did not have a car. I got her new car in an accident. It was a Honda Civic. It was totaled. I was blessed that I did not have major injuries. He had a car. The school officials called Annie to the school. She told them that she was having marital problems. They requested that she to go to a shelter. She did not want to accept the offer.

The next horrible thing he did was to stop paying his share Of the bills in the household. My sister did not make enough money at the time to pay all the bills, which included the mortgage. She could only pay essential bills such as water, gas, and electricity.

Ricky placed the house in foreclosure purposely. They were behind three months in mortgage. His goal was very vicious. He intended for Annie to lose the house if they got a divorce. The second outrageous thing he did was to quit his federal job. The purpose for this scheme was not to pay child support.

Annie's and my eyes stared up at God and said, "God, you are a higher power than mankind; You can take us through this. If we must go to a shelter temporarily, we must do it." We just humbled ourselves to the Lord. We had absolutely no savings in the bank. We reminisced about earlier in our lives, Annie and I as young adults around the age of twenty-three years old in Indianapolis, Indiana, going to the Salvation Army shelter in 1979. We were staying with my ex-husband's aunt. I got in an argument with her, because she was reading my mail when my husband was overseas in Africa. A big argument broke out. His aunt told us to get out of her house. We had nowhere to go but to a shelter.

When we arrived, there were women and children. Black and white people were at the Salvation Army. The women were battered by their husbands. One of the women staying there told us, "Girls, hold tight to your belongings; the people steal here." We slept on a folding Cot beside one another. They fed us three meals. We had to be in by 10:00 p.m. Luckily, my sister had some savings in the bank. We found an apartment in one week. Therefore, we had already experienced shelter life. We were willing to do it again. The only difference is that we had an eight- year-old child. It would have been difficult for him.

We listened to the scriptures every minister spoke to help us with this ordeal. One day, a pastor was talking about faith. The preacher said to walk by faith, not by sight (2 Corinthians 5:7). Therefore, we kept conditioning our minds to walk by faith, not by sight. We relinquished everything to God.

Ricky continued with his evil tactics. He made Junior write a letter to Annie, and it read, "I hate you. I want to live with Daddy.

Ricky and my sister were Summoned to a mediation hearing months before the court hearing in Miami Florida. The male attorney for my brother-in-law could not show up. A female attorney showed up. The male attorney for my sister was there.

Issues such as child support a nd housing were discussed between the two attorneys. The female attorney was a small built relatively young white American. Annie's attorney was African American.

The two attorneys got along Very well. It seemed very strange that the female attorney was supposed to be defending Ricky. It seemed like she went on the side of my sister's attorney. My sister's attorney told her that Ricky stopped paying bills. He showed her the nasty note from Junior, my nephew. Annie's attorney told her Ricky purposely made him miss school to make Annie look like an unfit mom.

Annie could see a serious 100k On the female attorneys face when her attorney presented these issues to her. Ricky told the female attorney that Junior was going with him. He had provided housing for him.

The female attorney abruptly spoke to Ricky in a harsh tone. She said, "Junior will stay with his mom. You will not take him anywhere." Then she also said, "You will be paying child support as stated in the decree. You will have weekend privileges." It was amazing to me, because she was supposed to be defending Ricky. Both attorneys turned against him. "No weapon formed against me shall prosper" (Isaiah 54:17). My sister's attorney recommended him to leave the house, because of the emotional impact he was having on Junior. The divorce was finalized on April 1, 1998. It was strange. It was April Fool's Day. Ricky had made a fool of himself.

When it came to moving, Ricky took his time to move. He moved from the house within three days when the mediation hearing concluded.

Ricky made sure he was going to leave Annie with nothing. Her situation was like Job in the bible. Job lost all his wealth, and he also lost his children. That is exactly what happened to Annie. She did not want to fight him over the materialistic things. She had faith; she would get these materialistic things back One must not put his trust in earthly treasures.

About the third day, Ricky went to the kitchen to pick up his utensils and things. There was some china he had purchased. He took the china and went to the back porch. He started throwing the china from the door on to the cement platform in the yard. He broke up all the new china. Annie and I said to one another, "What is he doing?" We called the police. The police said since he owned the china, he could break it. My sister said, "What if a kid gets cut?"

The police said, "That would be a civil matter with the child's family." Later, a big truck pulled up to the house. A friend of Ricky s helped him to move. Ricky moved out the living room furniture, dining room furniture, washer and dryer, Junior's video games, some Of Junioes clothes, Silverware, and the "Jesus

Later on, I heard from Junior, that Ricky had let Katherine store the "Jesus Clock" for him. She may have stored some other small things.

Ricky drifted around Miami for couple of days. Later, I found Out he moved to Philadelphia with his family.

Things at the house got harder and harder, because ofthe loss of the extra income. My sister got a loan to pay off the back mortgage. We decided to rent out the in-law quarters of the house. I worked part-time as a substitute teacher. I could not take a full-time shift, because of my medical problems.

Annie was able to purchase an Old 1988 Cavalier. It lasted for one year. It broke down. We found ourselves walking to the local grocery stores and to fast-food restaurants in the area for about three years. Neighbors drove by us and just waved to say "hello" to us. We caught taxicabs from the supermarket with groceries to home.

Creditors started harassing Annie about bills that were joined with Ricky. She did not have any money to pay them.

One school year, she did not have money to purchase Junior's clothes. A nice coworker purchased five outfits for her. God sent her an angel.

We ate whatever it took to fill our stomachs. We ate hotdogs, hamburgers, peanut butter, etc. This situation made us regress back to childhood. Our mom tried to raise us as best as she could on a social Security check.

Our faith got deeper and deeper. God was our friend. We never had a lot of friends from the start. But it ended up that it was just Annie and I going through this ordeal. The Bible says, "Wealth makes many friends. But the poor is separated from his friend" (Proverbs 19:4).

Annie was deeply saddened Over the turmoil with her husband and so-called friend. She told me at night, she would go to bed crying. She emphasized to me how she hated Katherine. But, later on, God healed her heart. She knew she could not hold hate since she was a Christian. Her blessing would have been hindered.

To sum it up, a household must stand on a solid rock. The husband is head of his household. He has to be strong. Satan enters through the head of the household. The husband has to institute values for his family. The husband is head of his wife as Christ is head Of the Church (Ephesians 5:22).

The husband can't let demon spirits enter in. Matthew 16:18 says, "On this rock, I will build my church and the gates of 'Hades' will not prevail against it." This is what a marriage must be like.

Malachi 2:14 says, "Yet, she is your companion and your wife by covenant. No man shall break this bond." God hates divorce, but God knew it would happen, because man can have a stone heart Or callous heart. This is what Ricky developed.

John 10:10 says, "The thief does not come except to steal and to kill and destroy. " This is what happened to my sister and Ricky.

To make this situation so bad, it was Annie's first marriage at the age of thirtynine years Old. She had been single for such a long while.

You must keep pressing on, no matter what situation comes your way. This Ordeal taught us strength and perseverance. In the Bible, James 1:2 says, "My brethren, count it all joy, when you fall into various trials, knowing that the testing of your faith produces patience. But let patience have its perfect work, that you may be perfect and complete, lacking nothing."

RENTERS AT "505"

My Sister, Annie, decided to rent out the in-law quarters Of the house. It was located in the rear of the house. She needed to rent to bring in more income since I was not able to work full time because Of my Stress level. It was her first time acting in a capacity of a landlord. We did not have family in town to move in our house to assist with the expenses.

We advertised Our property by placing "For Rent" signs on billboards in the local shopping area and On trees in our community. This was a practice the Haitians used to avoid paying for advertisement in the newspapers. The community Was predominately Haitian in 1997. There were very few African Americans in the area. She totally stepped out on faith.

We had no knowledge whatsoever about the Haitian culture. We knew they were one Of the largest black Caribbean groups in South Florida. We made a declaration to God: If He allowed us to hold on to the property, we would declare our house a house for the down and out to get on their feet. What we spoke out of our mouths came true. Everybody that rented had some type Of problem to solve and vision to accomplish. We charged cheap rent so that the renters could get on their feet.

All types of spirits entered "505." The renters were good and bad. Let me emphasize, there is good and bad in all cultures. God knew what we were getting into. All of the tenants paid their rent promptly, even though they had their ways.

Since my sister was a female running a house, she really caught it hard. She really had problems Out of the males, because they tried to run over her. Jacque was the first renter to come to the house to rent the in- law quarters in 1997.

Jacque was experiencing some personal problems. He owned property but rented it out because he'd been through a divorce. Jacque was of Haitian decent. He was about six feet tall and very dark-complected. Jacque's dream was to marry again and have a baby. He already had some grown children.

He moved in black and white furniture. We noticed he had a lot of black statues. These statues had ugly sculptured faces. We Were naive. We thought they were some kind of African art.

Jacque knew we were Christians. Jacque never went to church. He told us when evil came against him, he consulted a spiritualist. He handed us a business card for a spiritual adviser. We told him we believed in God, not man. Jacque did not believe in going to God with his personal problems. He always used the words "good" or "bad" when he referred to people. He was really helpful to us. We paid him to work around the house. If we needed a window placed, he would put it in for us. He would set out his trash and our trash.

He was very sociable and a giver. He would cook for his friends when they came to the house. If his friends needed money, he would lend them money.

But there Was a dark side to him we did not understand. It was a side that we did not understand, because We were born in an American culture that relied on Jesus Christ, not satanic practices to conquer evil spirits. He believed in buying different objects and placing them in his apartment. In Other words, he Was worshiping idols. The Bible says in Exodus 20:3-4, "You shall not have any Other gods before Me. You shall not make yourself a carved image—any likeness of anything that is in heaven above, or that is in the earth beneath, or that is in the water under the earth."

We got to know some Of the Haitian neighbors in the area. They knew of us because we were twins. Some of the neighbors told us his practice Was witchcraft. We were astounded. They told us the statues in his place were supposed to prevent evil people from hurting him. We told them this behavior was foolishness, and an object couldn't do anything for you. We took their belief for granted. Mentally, Jacque Saw the objects as giving him power to fight off evil. It just seemed so ridiculous to us.

Until I got to know what he was really doing, a lady pastor prayed Over me and revealed that she saw Witchcraft. I did not understand why she told me that. I had been in Africa. I thought since I lived in Africa, that was the reason she saw this practice around me. I did not understand why she kept saying it. I was also intelligent enough know that all Haitians did not believe in this practice. I saw so many Haitians going to the Catholic church right across the street from me.

Although everybody informed us about him, my sister could not kick him out. She needed the extra income. We were strong in our faith and felt that he could not hurt us. We felt that we had the victory in Jesus Christ. Palms 91:2 says, "I will say to the Lord, "He is my refuge and my fortress."

Later on, Jacque ran into a Jamaican lady who had been kicked out of her house by her family. He moved her into his place. He fell in love with her. A year later, she got pregnant with a baby girl. He Was a very happy man in the world. His female friend believed in God. She went to church with us on a couple of occasions. His dream came true. A baby was what he always talked about.

Jacque and his female friend moved back to his house. After a couple of years, he died in a horrible accident. He had a stick in his hand trying to pick an avocado from his tree. The branch of the tree was lying on the electric pole. He got electrocuted. We felt Sorry for him because he did not accept Christ.

We ran into a neighbor who knew him. "lhis lady told us Jacque had owed a lady some money. A lady went to a witchcraft person to work a spell on him. This was the reason the accident occurred. We told her this was insane talk. She was very persuasive about the matter.

Around 1999, the next tenant was a college girl. She was a beautiful Haitian about twenty-three years old. She was very pretty with a dark complexion. Her dream was to get married and become a nurse. She was attending college for nursing. Her name was

Marjorie. She was very respectable. She uras dating a gentleman who was studying to be a doctor.

She would cook Haitian dishes for us. The dishes were really healthy. They consisted Of vegetables and meats. We asked her about the practice of witchcraft. She told us this practice was performed mainly by the unintelligent Haitians. She did not believe in it.

She would tell us that everybody couldn't get an education in Haiti. Only the fortunate people with money could go to school. She said Some ofyoung people had to drop out Of school and go to work to support their families. She told us that some people can't afford to take care of their children if they have a lot of kids. A person may give a child away to a fortunate person to raise them. She also said, depending on the family, the child can be used as a maid to clean the person's house and cook. She also said if a young woman had looks, she could attract a well-off man, such as a doctor or a lawyer.

Her husband-to-be was very tall and handsome. He was of Haitian descent. They went to church every Sunday. They later got married. They invited us to their wedding. The wedding was beautiful.

Her husband obtained a position as an intern at a hospital in Missouri. She was a great person to have as a tenant.

Around the year 2000, a handsome Haitian guy, dressed very casually, came to the door with his wife and child who was about three years Old. The husband appeared to be blended into American culture for a number Of years. He spoke English very well and was gainfully employed at a fast-food restaurant. In addition, he was a college student. He looked about thirty-two years old. His name was Gregorie. His wife Was about twenty- Seven years old. They were seeking an apartment to rent. The in- law quarters of the house were vacant. His wife was wearing a white house dress. Her hair needed a perm. Her hair was sticking straight up in the air, like a porcupine's quills. She could have been an attractive girl if she had been dressed up. She looked like a country girl from overseas. Her name was Yvonne. She was a devoted Christian. She had been in the States for about one year.

She became Very impressed with the way we fixed our hair. My sister and I would weave our hair in a lot of fancy hairstyles. She started asking her husband to pay for her to get a weave. On Sundays, she would dress up prettily with pastel colors and go to church with her Son. Her husband never attended church.

Yvonne was your typical housewife. She cooked, cleaned house, and washed every day. My sister had to get on her about the washing. It seemed like an everyday task for her. It was raising my sister's water bill.

A year later, Yvonne became pregnant. She gave birth to a beautiful baby boy. The boy looked like his father.

Her husband told us he wished he could buy a house. He worked extra hours at the restaurant and worked at his cousin's night club for extra income. He told us since he was having another child, he needed more space.

He always admired the way Our house was built. Since we had an addition added on to the rear, we could bring in extra income. He wanted to find a house like ours.

God gave him his wish. He was able to find a house with an attachment. After he moved, we saw him a year later. He told my sister, "I want to thank you for charging me cheap rent. Because of you, I was able to get this house." My sister felt much appreciated, and she had performed a blessing in someone's life.

In the year 2001, a woman in distress was referred to us to rent a room in the front of our house. We rented her the smallest room, because it was cheap. She was going through a divorce and had nowhere to go. She needed immediate housing. Her name was Sabrina. She was of Haitian descent. She was a very intelligent lady. She was very cute. She had married a guy younger than she. She caught him talking on the phone with a girl in Haiti. This girl in Haiti was the one he really wanted to marry. He married Sabrina for citizenship. He was not in love with her. This was what caused the divorce.

Her dream was to get an apartment and be reunited with her son. He was taken away from her by the son's daddy. Sabrina had a lot of pain in her heart about her son. She did not get to bond with him. Her son'S father sent him to Turks Island in the West Indies to be raised with relatives.

This was her second marriage. She thought this marriage would work. She grieved over her second divorce.

Sabrina cooked very well, and she also cleaned very well. She would cook good Haitian dishes for us. She had a giving spirit. She would lend money out to her friends and family all the time. She was a bit flirtatious at times. When mechanics and gardeners came to the house, she would walk past them with a twist.

My sister Annie and I were on the plump side. I believe she thought her shape looked better than ours. Also, I believe Sabrina thought she was much prettier than us. Beauty is in the eyes of the beholder. She would talk to us a lot about what went on Haiti. Sabrina said that 50% of the people were Christians, and 50% of the people practiced witchcraft. She said that spirits ofwitchcraft, idolatry, and jealousy plagued the nation. For these reasons, so much oppression was on the people. She told us horrible stories about how people treated One another on the island. The spirit Of witchcraft existed heavily amongst the poor people. They believed in witchcraft to give them power to overcome anything.

She said if a person was jealous Of your prosperous business, the person would send someone t o burn your business down. She said that in families, a person could be jealous of his nephew if he was highly intelligent. If the nephew could become a prime minister, one of his jealous family members would have him killed.

She said that people in Haiti were scared of cats. When they heard a cat "meow," that meant evil. She said that her sister Was heavily into witchcraft to protect her bakery business. She said that neighbors did not bother her sister, because they were scared that she would work a spell on them.

Sabrina spoke of an occasion when a man tried to break into her sister's business and was killed by her sister's dogs. The police Came. They did not prosecute her sister. They moved the man's body. That was the end of that situation.

Sabrina also emphasized the evil and the good in people. She talked about a friend that owned a beauty parlor. Sabrina said the beautician would always fix her hair cheap. Sabrina said even if she did not have money, her beautician would fix her hair. She said that some ofthe Haitian people were jealous of her business. When she would go to work in the morning, roots were placed at her friend's door every day. The beautician would have to sweep away the roots every morning. Sabrina said the roots were used to destroy her business so that she would lose customers. Sabrina said her friend died in a car accident years later on the highway. She expressed how dearly she missed her friend. After she told us the story, it seemed so unrealistic.

Sabrina went to church with us on a couple of occasions. She would always talk about how so many preachers in the Haitian church were so hypocriticaL They were in it for the money. Therefore, she did not want to attend, because of hypocrisy. We told her to ignore the people. We told her these types of people were mentioned in the book Of Mathew 7:15: "Beware of false prophets that come to you in sheep' s covering, but inwardly they are ravenous wolves."

Finally, her son decided to come to America to go to college. She was elated. This was the first time since he was a baby that she was able to bond with her grown Son. She was tense all the time because she wanted to get a nice apartment for the two of

Sabrina decided to move from our house. But we found out there was a mysterious side to her.

On the day Sabrina was moving, she cleaned the room in our house thoroughly. We watched as she cleaned. We noticed she had a small broom under the bed. When I looked at the broom, I received cold chills down my arms. It just did not look like a normal broom that one would clean the house with. It looked like a witch's broom, a broom I saw as a little child in the movie, The *Wizard of oz*

We told her we did not like how the broom looked. It looked creepy. She said, "Why are you scared? This broom is used for brushing dust only." Her sister knocked at the door to assist with the move. She burst out laughing at us. She agreed that the broom was used for dusting. She demonstrated the broom by brushing off our ceiling fan in the living room. I asked a Haitian lady what the purpose of a broom under the bed was. She said the broom was used to control us and to protect the owner from evil spirits. Maybe Sabrina thought we Were going to take advantage of her, since we were twins. Maybe she was controlling us, and We did not realize it. I didn't know what to believe.

We called up a female pastor, Dr. Ruth Crockett, about this matter. She told us to get a bucket with bleach and mop the floor to run the evil spirits away. We adhered to her orders. In the year 2001, Peter, who was also of Haitian descent, came to the house to rent the in-law quarters in the rear of our house. We knew of him around the neighborhood, because his son used to play with my nephew, Junior. He had gone through a divorce and needed emergency housing W. e charged him $400.00 per month for rent. Utilities were included in the rent.

Haven't you heard that saying, "Never rent to people you know"? We really opened a Can of worms. He wanted a lot of privileges for $400.00.

Peter was about fifty-seven years old. He was not the most handsome man. He had a bald head. Peter spoke broken English. He was a very c lean person. He kept the apartment immaculate.

He worked a full-time job, as well as a part-time job. He did not make much money on his jobs. He would make up side jobs. He would buy all kinds of clothes and candies and re-sell the things overseas in Haiti. He stored barrels in his apartment with clothes to ship overseas. These were barrels from friends. He would charge them for storage.

To avoid buying dinner all the time, he would go to his friends to eat dinner free of charge. His friends would complain to us they were tired of him using them. When we would offer him food, he would walk off with the plate and spoon. We would ask for it back. peter would stall and say, "I forgot. "

We asked his friends, "Did he take your plates and spoons?" They Said, "Yes."

Peter would capitalize on us. We told him not to move an extra person in with him in the apartment. He would go ahead and move a roommate in. We would get on him a lot. He would not listen. Therefore, by moving a person in, his rent would be $200.00.

His friends used to tell us horror stories about Peter. I could not believe the things they would tell us. Peter talked about God and went to church every Sunday. I guess he liked to go to church, because he was a socializer, and he liked to get into people's business.

His friends told us he was a "Voodoo priest" in Haiti. We said, "What in the world is a Voodoo priest?"

A man told us a voodoo priest is a person that practices witchcraft. People in Haiti would go to this person as a spiritual adviser. If a person wanted a person killed because that person did evil to him, peter would work voodoo and get the person killed. He would get paid for the job. I don't know exactly what he did to the person. I don't know whether poison was placed in the person's food or whether an accident was set up. Maybe he surrounded himself with a lot of candles in prayer. The man told us he frequented the graveyards a lot in Haiti.

This sounded like something in a fairytale book to us. I said to the man, "l don't believe in any of the foolishness. Annie, Junior, and I are covered by the blood Of Jesus Christ. No weapon formed against us can prosper."

God revealed to us that he was really wicked when we told him to leave our house. We were tired of him taking advantage of us. We asked him to pay $50.00 more for rent. He did not want to pay it. We told him to move after two years, because he would not stick to policy. My sister wrote a letter asking him to move in August 2003.

Why did she do that? Chaos broke out at "505." He demanded his security deposit before he departed. He had a very stubborn, rebellious attitude. He wanted his security deposit of S400.00 back. Also, he wanted to be refunded for a car I sold him for

Annie kept telling him he would get his money. peter was determined he was going to get it.

When he did not get the money he requested, he broke the toilet. He made a $300.00 water bill.

My sister tried to get an eviction, but she did not have enough money to get one. She was overwhelmed with a lot of bills, and the process would have taken so long.

One day, he Came to the front of the house demanding all Of his money. My sister kept telling him, "I will give you your money when you move." He did not believe her.

He came at her with evil eyes and a tightened fice and looked like he wanted to hit her. My sister lost her temper and said, "You better get out Of my face. How many times are you going to get in my face?" She had had it with him taking advantage of us women. There Was a cup on the ground. She picked up the cup and tried to bust him in the head. I grabbed the cup from her quickly,

I said, "Are you crazy?"

Then Annie started speaking loudly, "Get away from me, Satan. You have no authority over me. Flee, Devil."

Peter ran to the other side of the house and called the police.

The police showed up. It was a Cop of Philippine origin and a Haitian American co p. I could tell that the Haitian American COP knew what Peter was trying to do but pretended he did not.

When Peter talked, he would swing his hands a lot. He accidentally touched the Philippine cop. The Cop knew that he was trying to take advantage Of us, because my sister showed him a letter requesting peter to leave. She showed him the water bill that Peter had made. She told him about the car he wanted the refund on. The cop asked Peter, "Did you hit me? Because if you tried to hit me, I am going to take you down now."

Peter nervously said, "No.

Also, the cop threatened him. He said, "If you don't get out of their house, I will throw you out myself." I knew that the cop was sent in the form of a guardian angel. The cop told him, "Man, you do not deserve a refund on a car you purchased. You will have to wait for your security deposit like she says."

My sister kept reading the Bible daily for a revelation on how to resolve this matter with this evil tenant. She came across a verse in Acts 19:12. The Apostle Paul placed handkerchiefs or aprons on the sick to expel the diseases, and the evil spirits departed out of them. So, we decided that we would spiritually use this biblical verse to expel peter out of our house.

What we did was we went to the store and purchased some handker chiefs and took scissors and Cut them in half. We placed the handkerchief at the rear of the house that led to the-in-law quarters where peter stayed. We Went to the inside of the in-law quarters and placed handkerchiefs under his couch, under his mattress, and in his closet.

When he came back to his apartment, we went into the bedroom close to the in-law quarters and prayed. We prayed loudly. "Satan, leave this house, in the name of Jesus." It was so loud I knew the Other neighbors heard us. Peter was gone in two days. I knew it was a combination of two things: the faith that was in us and the guardian cop that came that day.

I can honestly Say he was the Worst tenant We had at "505." But God delivered us from him.

MAINTENANCE HELPERS AT "505"

Since my sister and I were single with a child, we had to rely On male help to keep the house in order, for example, painting, fixing broken things such as locks, and positioning furniture in the house.

The helpers came from lower socioeconomic levels. Some of them were in a worse financial situation than We were.

Our first long-time helper was a roofer. The real state company referred him to us in 1995. He was a dark-skinned Haitian. His name was Willie. He worked on our roof from the time my sister purchased her house. We had a preblem with minor leaks occurring in the addition attached onto the house. He would fix the leaks. When he fixed a leak, it lasted for two years at least. He was an expert in the field.

He Owned a small business. He v,ras very generous and helped individuals who had problems. My sister did not have a lot of money after her divorce. When he performed a job for you, you could pay him partial payments until you finished the debt.

He trusted us for some reason. I guess he felt sorry because we were women with a Child. He complained to us that some people tried to cheat him out of his money when he finished their repairs.

We could always rely on him to show up, even if he knew that he would not get all ofhis money. I know that was God placing him in our lives.

One day, there was a knock at the door. A black gentleman stood there dressed in a T-shirt and blue jeans. A bike stood at   his side. When he opened his mouth, we noticed he had a stutter. He said, "May I Cut your yard for $25.00?"

I paused a while and called my sister to get the okay. Annie jumped on the deal, because that was cheap to cut a large yard like ours.

We started calling him the "Stutter." We found out he was disabled. His name was Wallace. My sister and I felt sorry for him, because Wallace told us he got shot at thirty-two years old. It was something foolish that disabled him. He got shot over talking to a female in her house. The female's boyfriend walked in while they were talking. This was such a young age for another person to take your health away.

We gave him jobs now and then. The jobs included painting, fixing locks, laying tile rugs, etc. What I admired about him was he was willing to work to supplement his Social Security check. He did not want to sit home and have a lazy attitude looking at television all day.

During his rounds in several neighborhoods, he would find things people threw out, for example, chairs, tables, glasses, etc. He would retrieve the things and try to sell them to other less fortunate people at a cheap price. One day, he came to us with a Bible. It was in Spanish. I said to Wallace, "I can't speak Spanish." Therefore, he just gave it to us. So, we found someone to give it

When my sister had extra money, she would give him more money to do things around the house. Her conscience bothered her if she worked him too cheap. Sometimes, he would get into a daze for a couple Of minutes and just glance out into the street. I assumed he was asking God, "Why did this have to happen to me?"

My sister suffered with getting all the wood around her house repaired, because it was too expensive for a roofer to do. Willie, the roofer, did not have all the manpower to invest. She kept praying to God, saying, "l I would get my wood changed."

One day, we were sitting in Burger King. Right across from of us were two white Americans that we often saw in Burger King. Their brother walked in the door. so, one of the brothers told us, "If you wonder why his clothes looks soiled like that all the time, he does roofing work."

We said, "Oh really?"

When the soiled brother sat down, my sister asked him how much he would charge to change the wood around an entire house.

He said, "Not much." His name Was Randy. It was truly a blessing. He changed the wood on the entire house for $1500.00. The work was really worth $5000.0(). He was the second roofer placed in our lives.

Randy was a really interesting person. Society would have seen him as a homeless person, because Of the way he looked. He worked hard every day. He did not worry about what society thought of him. He wanted to live a humble life in the country. He did not worship money as a god. He even said if he won the lotto, he would help poor people.

Sometimes, he would feed the homeless people at Burger King with the hard-earned money he worked for.

He had been through a lot of trials in life. We would spread the gospel to him. He would listen, but I knew he questioned God at times. One day, he came to the house mad about a personal matter. He looked up in the sky and said, "God show yourself. Everybody talks about You. Show Yourself to me. I am not scared of You."

When he said that, I told him not to threaten God like that. Something can happen to you. I prayed to God when he left that he would not get hit by a car riding his bike.

I can sum it up by saying, "He who has pity on the poor lends to the Lord. And he will pay back what he has given" (Proverbs 19:17). Our behavior constituted this character. This is why God sent helpers all the time.

Even though they had their share Of trials, we did not turn our face in another direction. In fact, we tried to spread the gospel to them. They either accepted it or relied on themselves for help. We encouraged them to walk by faith, not by sight, because this is exactly what we were doing.

OVERALL VIEW OF RENTING AT "505" AFTER THE CHRISTIANS AND DEMONS LEFT.

Good spirits as well as bad spirits entered "505," spirits of jealousy, covetousness, idolatry, and enviousness. Actually, spirits Of the human flesh entered. Christians and demons lived in our household.

It's always good to talk about positive things before talking about negative things. We Were blessed that the Haitians paid their rent On time. They really had standards about paying their rent on time. They knew shelter in this country was a necessity. It was a blessing, because Our house would have gone into foreclosure without their help. We also helped them, by giving them cheap rent.

The Haitians taught us economic means Of survival, and we really got a good education. Annie and I were wasteful spenders, even though we did not have a lot Of money. To save on electricity, the Haitian renters cut their lights off in the daytime. We would have a tendency to leave ours on.

The Haitians did not like to u se dryers. They hung their clothes on the line. They said the dryer would deplete the texture of the material. We always used our dryer.

Furthermore, the Haitians did not like to eat out a lot at restaurants and go to carry-outs. The women were very domestic, and they cooked a lot. The meals were very nutritious. The meals included a lot Of vegetables and fruits.

Instead of drinking sodas, they drank fruit drinks, such as pineapple and mango juice. In addition, they loved to bake their cakes from scratch, instead Of buying an already-made cake from the supermarket.

They made household income by doing all kind of things. If a person owned a van, they would make income by taking a person to work. There would be a carload Of four to five people in a van.

The people did not have to necessarily work at the same place.

What amazed me was how some Of the Haitians salvaged things from Street corners and had them repaired. For example, if Someone threw Out a mattress, they would have it cleaned. I saw them picking up refrigerators that neighbors had thrown out. I assumed they knew an electrician to fix it.

What can one do with milk cartons and jars? I saw them pick them up from the streets. I hear that they shipped them overseas to Haiti to relatives.

When it came to renting in their households, they rented to family and friends from overseas to keep the mortgage going. If a tenant did not have a telephone and wanted to use the landlord 's telephone, they charged the person for the phone call, even if it was for a local call. In addition, if the tenant needed to use the washer, they would charge the tenant a fee, just like going to the washhouse.

If a Haitian household had a large living room, they would split the room in half by using sheet rock for an extra bedroom.

The women were very domestic. They cooked dinners and sold them from their house to bring in extra money.

My Haitian roommate told me when some of the Haitians needed to buy a house, they would get a credit card. They would charge a down payment against their credit card. I thought this was very smart, depending on what the interest rate on the credit card was, because it is very hard to save for a house nowadays.

I found the business skills very remarkable, and we took note of them for Ourselves.

The demonic Haitian tenants believed in witchcraft, but we were not so naive that some of them were trying to practice witchcraft on us. We found out that they had a very controlling nature. When my sister told them not to do things, they went ahead anyway, even though they were not the owners of the property. It was control that manifested in a lot of mental games. Mental games come with lies to manipulate.

1 Samuel 15:23 says, "For rebellion is as the sin of witchcraft." But we were covered by the precious blood of Jesus Christ. They did not have victory over us.

We heard all kinds of beliefs from the people that practiced witchcraft. One neighbor told us that every day, she bleached her porch to fight off evil spirits from entering and attacking her family. She told us We should do it. I said, "l don't believe bleach can do anything but clean your house."

Some of the tenants manifested jealous spirits. If you purchased furniture, their face would tighten. On one occasion, we purchased a small television for the kitchen. Thank God, it was used. The television worked for two weeks, and it came up broke. I believe my female roommate, Sabrina, did something to it.

Since I was not working a full-time job, one of our roommates would purposely make the bathroom junky to make me work harder around the house. Again, this is a sign of control.

Remember, you people, evil cannot overtake you. Psalms 91:10 says, "No evil shall befall you. Nor shall any plague come near your dwelling."

Even though we had our ups and downs, renting was a learning experience. There is goo d and bad in all cultures. But the bad things may be presented in another fashion.

I WAS USED AS A "VESSEL"

Even though I was not gainfully employed because my case was in litigation with the Social Security Administration for disability benefits, I believe God used my life to be a vessel to mankind. My spirit poured out on the poor, like blood running through a vessel in my body.

My acquaintances were in worse financial shape than me. Some of them did not have support from their family. My sister, Annie, stuck to me like wallpaper glued to a wall. Some of them did not have family to give them hope, faith, and courage.

One day, I was walking to the grocery store. I saw a lady standing Outside the store begging for food. The shoppers passed by her, and they ignored her. She said to me, "I am hungry. Could you buy me some food?" She was dressed in a white blouse and blue shorts to her knees.

I told her, "I do not have money, but I will buy you some food off my food stamps. I don't work. I have little money."

The lady responded, "God bless you!"

I went into the store and purchased a large bag of chicken and some canned goods. I found out her name was Gloria. She was on Social Security disability. Her money from her check would run out before the end of the month.

We exchanged telephone numbers. Gloria would call to say hello often. She always had a problem with not having enough money. I tried to help her the best way I could. Sometimes, she needed a ride to the grocery store. I would use my sister's car and drive over fifty blocks to get her. I exhausted my sister's gas to get her.

Some of my friends would call about their personal problems. I truly had my own to worry about. Some of them were having marital problems. Their husbands were cheating on them. I offered them spiritual counseling and invited them to church with me.

I was able to relate to their situation, because I was going through my personal problems with lack. But, sometimes, some Of my friends placed so much pressure on me, I did not understand why, because they knew I was not working full time. It seemed as though they thought I could perform miracles for them. I don't know whether they thought I had it made, because my sister had a good federal government job.

Jesus said in the Bible, "You have the poor always, but me you do not have always." I believe God placed these individuals in my life to give them hope to go On, even though their situations looked bleak.

From the perspective of the world, my life may have looked insignificant after my divorce, but I believe God used me tremendously to support my sister, Annie, and nephew, Junior. Annie was a single mom trying to manage a household.

I was there at the house when the repairmen Came. I opened the door for the roofer, the air-conditioning man, the plumber, and the handyman many times. Annie would have had to schedule leave from work to take care of these matters.

I was like a second mom to my nephew, Junior. I took him to his doctor's appointments in early childhood. I made frequent visits to the pediatrician. I was home when Junior stayed home sick from school. I was there to pick Junior up from aftercare at school.

In pre-adolescence, I counseled him as well as his mother about not getting involved in teenage crime, such as gangs on the streets, and I counseled him about drug usage amongst teenagers.

I took care of personal business for Annie a lot. If she needed a package picked up from the post office, I was there to get it. If she needed me to go to Home Depot for things for the house, I Was there to do it.

I was there to take care Of the family laundry, clean the house, and to run to the grocery store for my family.

The Bible says in Romans 8:28, "And we know that all things work together for good to those who love God, to those who are the called according to His purpose." I believe I served my purpose for my sister and Junior.

CONCLUSION: PRAYER AT LEISURE MOMENTS

Since I was out of work full time for at least fifteen years, all I could do was pray to keep my sanity. I constantly wrote notes to God asking for a miracle. In the book of Habakkuk 2:3, it says, "Then the Lord answered me and said: "Write the vision, And make it plain on tables, That he may run who reads it. For the vision is yet for an appointed time." In the Bible, Hebrews talks about faith. Hebrews 11:1 says, "Now faith is the substance Of things hoped for, the evidence ofthings not seen." In the Bible, it Says in John 14:13, "And whatever you ask in My name, that I will do, that the Father may be glorified in the Son. If you ask anything in My name, I will do it." The more I prayed, the more it looked like nothing would happen. I believe God placed me in a valley, because I had to learn about Him and have a deeper relationship with God. I learned about going through trials and tribulations, such as losing everything, a job, personal shelter, the eb44ty to visit lavish restaurants, and all types of Arabic- and European-style hotels. Now, I realized what Jesus went through leaving the Gold Mansion in Heaven to come down to earth to save mankind. It was a sacrifice to come down to earth and die on the cross at Calvary for Our sins. The humility always remained in me, because I never had selfish ambitions, nor was I conceited. I always thought about helping mankind. Humility really became known to me, because I was at Jesus' feet. I sought the Lord. I feel like the lady with the issue Of blood for twelve years in the book of Mark chapter 5, verse 25. She ran behind Jesus and touched his garment. She begged for healing. I had to depend on medication for fifteen years. Could one imagine, if Jesus came to town, everybody would be running to him.

I had to learn how to forgive my ex-husband, Coco, for what he put me through. At one time, I felt hatred in my heart against him.

God took it away. God revealed to me humility is not selfishness. You have to surrender resentment.

Since these trials, I have been given a relationship with people and their problems. I had to learn to have a positive tongue. I realize God can bring you up and take you down if you don't serve him in the proper way. Daniel 4:37 (c) says, "Those who walk in pride He is able to put down. " I feel my situation was like Job in the Bible; he lost everything. God gave it back to him. I know the feeling of being poor and how it felt. I have sympathy with the poor, because I was at the food stamp line at HRS (Health Rehabilitative Services). Earlier in my life, I was dining out at the best restaurants in the world. I got frowns from the HRS workers when I came in for assistance. They had arrogant looks on their faces. Isaiah 61:7 says, "Instead of your shame you shall have double honor, And instead of confusion they shall rejoice in their portion." Friends called the house to get in my business or didn't call at all. It is an honor to sit here to write this book, because someone in the world can relate to my situation. This is a childhood dream come true in my life. I hope Thick As Glue will change your life and give you hope to go on. It is a privilege to tell the world what one missionary went through leaving the field I. don't know what happened to the Other missionaries that came back to America. I'm sure they too have a Story to tell.